HAND-FASTING: A PRACTICAL GUIDE

Hand-fasting:
A Practical Guide

By
Mary Neasham

GREEN
MAGIC

This first edition published in 2003 by
Green Magic
Long Barn
Sutton Mallet
Somerset TA7 9AR
England

Typeset by Academic and Technical, Bristol
Printed by Antony Rowe, Devizes

Cover design by Chris Render
Cover artwork © Alison Hall 2003
Technical assistance by Rose Gotto and Tania Lambert

ISBN 0 9542963 1 1

GREEN MAGIC

Contents

Acknowledgements

My biggest thanks must go to my daughter Gemma and her loved one Andy for their maturity and understanding throughout the time it has taken me to write this book, not least during the last few weeks as I have been recovering from an unfortunate riding accident, and they have looked after me brilliantly.

With deep love and understanding I wish to thank my mother, for without her support (and she knows what I mean) I couldn't possibly have written either of my books to date. Thanks mum!

I also wish to thank Anna de Benzelle for being both my co-writer on *Teenage Witch's Book of Shadows* and one of my original mentors, offering her invaluable common-sense advice to my constant requests for enlightenment on particular subjects despite her hectic schedule.

Grateful thanks must be given to Harry Baldock for being my 'other' mentor over the past few years, for his never-ending support of my work, and friendship that I hugely appreciate—and for constantly coming to my rescue!

Thank you to Dolores for your transatlantic perspective on all I do.

I wish to thank Jenny for her friendship and positive encouragement and proving that old ways can meet new age and find common ground. Thanks also to David for always being there and offering your unique perspective and wisdom. To Liz, my oldest friend, for our continued journey together, not to mention that wonderful fortieth birthday present last year, I say thank you!

Many thanks to Oakilia for the copy of her ceremony and continued support of Coppice Craft.

I thank Kathy Jones for her input—I know we haven't met as yet but I hope we do soon.

And lastly to Chris and Pete for supporting my endeavours so enthusiastically!

Introduction

My lover in the corn field doth stand
My husband guides the plough
My children work from dawn to dusk
Our strength it will withstand.

My love is elusive as the moon
My face doth reflect her light
My marriage is the midday sun
Our harvest will be soon.

My husband knows my lover's mind
My heart belongs to both
My children are my only hope
Our fertility from the land.

(Anon)

Marriage as an institution is both fascinating and yet elusive in its true origins—it remains a mystery. For thousands of years men and women have been going through marriage ceremonies for a variety of reasons. It is easy in these liberal times to think of marriage as a romantic ideal rather than a necessity. All over the world people are getting married for reasons other than romance—some marry for love, some due to pregnancy, some for financial reasons (good and bad), some marriages are arranged and all are legally binding except pagan ceremonies.

Whilst researching and subsequently writing on this subject, I had to consider the many varied people it could reach. For this reason I have tried to approach the subject in a manner that I hope will suit both the highly initiated and the average layman. My humble apologies in advance if you feel this is not achieved and my grateful thanks if you feel it is.

As I finish this little book my best friend has rung me to invite me to her wedding in two weeks' time. They are an established couple who have been together now for eight years. 'This will be a low key affair', she informed me. 'No gifts and no hats, definitely no hats', we laughed. Hers is not a traditional romantic wedding but a marriage of mutual financial convenience to both. Their love is not in question here nor is their suitability, for I cannot think of a more committed pair! These days, however, people may look a little stunned at how informally they are taking it, but judge not. Many an over-romanticised wedding can end in tears a few years down the line with couples growing apart rather than together.

I set out to write a simple little book on hand-fastings and found myself entrenched in the history of marriage generally. The two are intrinsically linked throughout history, as I discovered, and in so doing I hope I have shed some light on our joint British and Celtic pasts.

Personally I feel that today's pagan ceremonies are perfectly entitled to take the best from the past and integrate it with the ideals for the future and, if anything, modern hand-fastings are possibly the most emotive and romantic weddings you are likely to attend. Due to my own limited experiential involvement in hand-fastings to date, I enlisted help from a wide variety of people during my research, ranging greatly in their chosen paths. The one thing all my interviewees had in common, regardless of tradition, was that they all agreed the couple should design their day themselves as much as possible.

The role of today's pagan priesthood in modern hand-fastings seems to be firstly that of spiritual guidance, secondly to be present to officiate or act as celebrant and, lastly, if needed, to raise loving spiritual energy and invoke deities if required rather than attempting to inflict any autocratic control over the couple. This is well demonstrated in the copies of service orders included in later chapters. These are services that were worked out in advance, with couples deciding on the actual wording, whilst priestesses and priests like myself guided them, if required, through any traditional practices applicable to the path they tread. This level of input and control is becoming very attractive to people from all walks of life as most modern services, whether church or civil ceremony, are far less flexible in their approach. The binding of the couple's hands is optional in some traditions and not even mentioned in others, but many different paths have since adopted it from its original Celtic past.

Modern ceremonies are a glorious conglomeration—partly following ancient customs but also adapting to new spiritual philosophies both universally and personally.

As a race we are unique in the way we continually try to define our intimate relationships, finding new and beautiful ways with which to express and display our love. Hand-fasting ceremonies allow the couple to bare their souls in any way they so wish, encouraging us to use our imaginations to their fullest.

The ceremony itself can often provoke strong emotions for all but the most sceptical and cynical. Sadly we, in the West, live in a world of superficial consumerism lead by market forces rather than any long term plan of global love, tolerance and ecological sustainability for our children to inherit. We will pay the price for this short-term fix, as will Mother Earth. Our only hope seems to be to allow the dance of the GOD and GODDESS to be recognised so that love and acceptance of all life take on deeper meanings for us. I personally feel that the achievement of global and intimate spiritual love should be the goal we all aim for in life.

Hand-fastings are a step towards honest loving relationships where couples can put their spiritual selves on a higher plane, with their other needs simplifying as a result of this ritual. By living a more loving and spiritual path couples will strengthen, within and without, coping with any tests the universe throws their way, and hopefully relegating consumerism to a much lower level of importance.

There are no 'right' or 'wrong' ways of hand-fasting, but love is expected to be deep, honest and true—as is a certain level of spiritual understanding and/or awareness. The popular slang of hand-fastings is an interesting derivative of hand-fastenings which most of the elder generation I have consulted over the writing of this book agree on, but no one seems to know how or why they became hand-fastings. I haven't come across any specific pre-wedding fasting prior to the event, and fastening or binding does in fact make far more sense—but for the sake of these modern times and to save confusion I will refer to them as hand-fastings.

Groom

Under the moonlight I'll embrace you
With all my heart I'll love you
My body will know such ecstasy
As it is to be with you.

Bride

Under the sun I'll feel your strength
With my spirit I'll love you
My soul will know such ecstasy
As it is to be with you.

(Example of vows from modern hand-fasting)

1

History

Like many other ancient British customs and traditions, the origins of hand-fasting are hard to pin down with any degree of chronological accuracy. From the remaining evidence it seems possible that early Britons, prior to any invading forces, practised their own form of pagan worship and therefore rites of passage including marriages. Historians debate the validity of an actual Celtic migration from mainland Europe into Britain, but the geological evidence for our physical attachment as recently as 7000 before common era tends to give it credence.

To discover whether hand-fastings or a version of them existed prior to recorded history we have to turn to archaeology.

Mankind began to give up its nomadic lifestyle after the retreat of the last ice age, and it is then that we have the first signs of animals being domesticated and early agriculture emerging. This occurred at about 8000 BCE, reaching our shores around 5000 BCE. From the stone age and up until the end of the bronze age, communities were thought to be sexually equal—and if anything women were probably held in higher esteem due to their reproductive ability. Many feel that this was essentially a goddess-worshipping matriarchal society. Birth was a highly dangerous time for both mother and child, with mortality rates high for both. It is thought that couples would require permission from the gods before having children, and any decision taken by the local priest would be judged on the families' and community's ability to provide for an extra mouth.

By expediting weaning with the introduction of milk gruel made from milk and ground grain, they could get babies off their mothers' breasts quickly. Two advantages arose from this: children grew faster and would be able to work the land in some way or another by the age of three, and by ceasing breast-feeding earlier than normal the woman's fertility would increase.

They built houses for the first time and accumulated property including domestic livestock. All this became something that could be handed down to the next generation, thus beginning the tradition of inheritance. By agreeing to actively breed so intensively they became very vulnerable. It was fairly easy to protect one baby or small child, but if you had a cluster of youngsters to consider this put the whole community in a more perilous position if invaded. Prior to the early settlements of the bronze age, a small nomadic group if attacked only had to defend itself or run away. Now there was nowhere to run, and defending themselves became defence of livestock and property also, so it was more of an issue than it had been before. Men largely took this role of guardians and protectors, which was by and large a natural evolution of the time. Only those women not pregnant or breastfeeding would join ranks with the men to fight if needs be, and gradually we see evidence for the subordination of the matriarchal society to the patriarchal one we still live in today.

Marriage may have been celebrated previously but now it had new significance. It became a contract introduced to strengthen the group or community. This happened for a variety of reasons: the interests of any children born to a couple would be protected; couples would be expected to take the relationship more seriously; and for political and economic gain. Sadly, viewed with hindsight, it appears that women basically became goods and chattels to be bartered.

Considering the free and easy way in which people of then and now marry, breed and part it makes some sense—or does it?

We are so used to living in our modern society of rules and regulations, laid down by elected governments, guided by science, that it is easy to forget the strong spiritual past we all belong to. This is our mutual pagan and heathen past in which society was ruled by the witness of neighbours and families, and was judged by priests whose spiritual knowledge and understanding was not to be questioned by commoners.

The earliest evidence in Britain for an established Neolithic settlement is at Scara Bay on Orkney. This includes houses with the burial pits of the families that lived there, and the Ring of Brodgar (a stone circle nearby) which may have been used for marriage ceremonies amongst other things. The people who lived there were Picts and it's thought they could have been some of the earliest settlers from Scandinavia. Once our ancestors decided to settle and farm, their life style changed through the newly enforced circumstances. Although only small family groups initially, they would meet up seasonally with other family groups to trade, feast and pair off. Once these groups decided to put down roots they joined up and established larger multi-family societies and founded the first villages.

The earliest marriage ceremonies were business contracts between parents, entered into to increase security through the wealth, status and protection of the families concerned. This situation has been the norm for thousands of years in many parts of the world—India, for example, has arranged marriages, which have continued to this day, and purely romantic weddings are definitely seen as modern incursions from the West, ironically.

The Vikings and Henry VIII largely destroyed our most ancient monastic libraries that might have provided more clues, so it is to the unreliable and essentially biased Roman documents that we have to turn for some of our evidence.

The Julius work calendar is an excellent insight into the everyday life of the British peoples of this time, but to glean information of our Celtic and pre-Celtic past we have to rely on modern archaeology. It is the archaeology of long barrows, standing stones, hillside chalk figures and domestic items that demonstrate an organised society of clans in the north and tribes farther south. They held strong beliefs and respected their local and national deities, whilst trying to live in harmony with nature. They began to bury their dead ritualistically. These must have been strange and difficult times to live in with food and shelter still taking precedence. Marriage came way down the list of priorities.

As these early settlers evolved into more sophisticated societies they developed rituals and traditions for all occasions, but death whether natural or sacrificial still held pole position. This newly enforced interference into people's romantic lives came with its own share of problems for, in attempting to exert control over love, rebellion was obviously going to occur. Infidelity was just as prolific then as it is now, but punishments were far harder to bear for those caught.

Looking back at the original Celtic way of life I think it likely that the richer lords and ladies of the time did have some sort of initiated Druid ceremony, but it's unlikely that the majority did anything more than have a small celebration if they could afford it.

Modern hand-fastings seem to owe their presence to far simpler affairs that took place, in some form or another, all over the British Isles. The earliest recorded ones took place in medieval Scotland at around the same time as the introduction and subsequent establishment of the Celtic Catholic church. Previous to this, hand-fastings amongst the Celts of Scotland and Ireland were believed to be recognition of betrothal, not marriage. A couple considering marriage would become engaged, usually at Beltane or May Day, seen as a time associated with romance. They didn't need witnesses, although this helped, and would normally announce their engagement, not marriage, at this stage. Any couple entering into a sexual relationship could be considered married by the community, betrothed or not, although this wasn't always easy to prove. Back in those times couples wishing to become married could do so legally by stating that they were married to each other, without any need for a ceremony. As with betrothal, this could take place with or without any witnesses, and a priest was not required. Some would choose to ask one, but they were mostly the rich, as the poor couldn't usually afford such services. Villages and towns all over the British Isles have special and secret sites traditionally associated with this practice, from ancient trees to waterfalls, where couples have declared their love for one another. The custom of hand-fasting for a year and a day came later still, and probably derives from the Scottish inheritance laws which forbid any spouse to inherit their deceased partner's wealth unless they had been married for at least a year and a day. If a child had been born within this time period, then the estate passed on to the offspring. This law still stood until 1940!

If a couple decided to have a hand-fasting marriage ceremony this would consist of whomever they wanted to attend. There were no set procedures to follow and only very basic rules. Hand-fasting in its simplest form could just be a confirmation of love and commitment between the couple concerned, acknowledged by the community as a marriage unless it broke one of the few laws it fell under. One law was that they must not be too closely related, another was that neither party was committing bigamy, and lastly marriage was disallowed between under-aged couples, 12 years for girls and 14 years for boys.

Strong opposition from the respective families had a similar bearing on the couple as it does today, but if living in an early bronze age settlement it would have been very difficult to bear, with opposing 'in laws' living in such close proximity.

If one of the couple's parents approved then the family could expect to lose their offspring to this family, something that might have dire consequences. Losing an adult male meant the loss of heirship, protection and work, whereas losing a female meant the loss of grandchildren and literally severing a branch from the family tree. I like to think that the politics of relationships haven't changed that much over the past few thousand years, and most couples would if pushed or provoked just end up living with or near whichever branch approved more and gave the least grief to them. The same applies today if we think about it—love and marriage hasn't changed a great deal over the past few thousand years: people are still people. Earlier in the British Isles matrimony experienced many changes, with each invading force bringing its own traditions.

The Romans bought their own customs and ceremonies, essentially pagan but biased towards city life. The hierarchy was not encouraged to marry natives unless it was of huge political benefit. Roman citizens were supposed to marry within their own social class; slaves could not officially marry and the groom's fathers arranged most Roman marriages. It is thought that the Romans invented the idea of a wedding dowry given to the groom on receipt of his bride, but Celts and Vikings and later Anglo-Saxons also practised this in various forms. The financial incentive gave the couple a chance to establish their marriage and invest in their future. Dowries continued to be exchanged as a matter of course among the middle and upper classes in this country until about two hundred years ago, with some families still continuing a similar practice today. Both my ex-husband's family and my own gave us a lump sum to help us on our way, enabling us to put a deposit down on a house and buy furniture. This unexpected surprise was very welcome, but shows how some of us still have the old traditions deeply ingrained in us.

Roman life, however, centred on Rome and the prestige attached to becoming a Roman citizen. Even when abroad they continued to exist under the strict rules inflicted upon them from the senate in Rome. Female citizens enjoyed slightly higher status than their Greek counterparts and could own property and trade. Marriage ensured stability and the emphasis was on producing pure Roman citizens, preferably male. The women of Rome were far from stupid, though, and like their Greek cousins took to using herbal contraceptives to exert some control over childbearing. Ironically pomegranate, the sacred plant of the goddess Aphrodite, was a favourite for such practices. This fruit was also used in Hebrew marriage ceremonies and the couple would jump on it to symbolically release its fertility, although figs were also used.

These ancient Mediterranean times had very different attitudes towards love and romance, from what we know of ancient Greece and Rome. Mediterranean men were frequently bisexual and more likely to fall in love with their mates than with their wives, who were for a while really used just for breeding and domestic duties. From what we can tell, Greeks and Romans had major fears of female sexuality whereas, as far as we know, for the Celts, Norse, Saxons and Normans this wasn't a major issue. Then, around 200 BCE, the Romans turned full circle and faced what they feared most, embarking on an era of female adoration with heterosexuality and the female orgasm being the highest aspiration, something they may have learnt from the Celts.

Goddess statues popped up everywhere and worship of female divinity was embraced both spiritually and physically. In their wedding vows, however, they remained patriarchal by introducing the concept of obedience from their spouse. Rome underwent radical changes religiously and by tolerating the Christian influence initially they inadvertently let it in through the back door. Seeing themselves as scholars and intellectuals, Romans accepted the new theology for the large part although some of the Emperors objected to the new Judaism referring to Christ the Lord instead of the Emperor. Eventually conversion took place and the deaths of so many Christian martyrs only strengthened its power. By 400 CE Rome became the self-appointed head of Western Christianity and had a Pope as its focal point. Between 400 and 500 CE monks or missionaries, largely funded by Rome, were spreading out all over Europe and attempting to convert pagans from their heathen beliefs.

Britain had largely recovered from its previous Roman invasions and the Celtic tradition was enjoying its own resurrection. Christianity slipped in through missionaries and monasteries infiltrating our land, and a strange era of bending and blending took place. One wonders if the subsequent invasion of Germanic tribes to Britain was partly to escape the spread of Christianity in mainland Europe. This could also apply to the Vikings, who would have had more in common religiously with pagan Celts than with Christians.

The Anglo-Saxons did deals over marriage, but the emphasis was on strengthening tribal groups and the trade that could then result from such unions. They actively encouraged inter-tribal weddings and many Celts became absorbed into Saxon life this way.

The Vikings arrived with their own traditions relating to marriage and, as already mentioned, they dealt in dowries for much the same reasons as pre-Christian Romans had. Viking men were supposed to provide for their families and any husband found failing in this department could find himself being divorced and excommunicated from his tribe. His wife was then free to look elsewhere for a more reliable spouse. This divorce law goes back over a thousand years but to some extent still applies today. Viking ceremonies would probably have been similar to Celtic or Druid practice, but using different pantheons of gods and goddesses. The Vikings have received bad press over the years and were thought to be a marauding force of barbarians hell-bent on raping and pillaging indiscriminately. Personally I don't entirely believe this, I feel they were the last pagan stronghold in Europe at the time and they saw the British Isles as a retreat and possible sanctuary. Looking at the evidence of their sporadic attacks they focused primarily upon established Christian monasteries and churches. This I feel was more of a religious war than a simple booty run. These were harsh, bloody and desperate times for the old Norsemen and women and we were possibly their last resort.

The Normans were obviously Christian and their marriage ceremonies were similar in many respects to those of today. There was more concern over the virginity and purity of the bride but marriages were still for the large part arranged affairs. This was, in part, a romantic era of knights in shining armour and damsels in distress. Surprisingly, many of our views on romance probably stem from these times: particularly, it seems entrenched in the female psyche. How many women today hold on to the romantic notion of a knight rescuing them from whatever dilemma they are in and sweeping them off their feet? As a reader of the tarot I can tell you, most of them do! We still think of this as the birthplace of romance with men fighting valiantly over the honour of the lady. It's easy to get carried away with images of beautiful maidens in flowing medieval gowns dropping their favour to their favourite knight as he runs the gauntlet for her or jousts on horseback. Think of the sheer number of legends and films that have derived from these times, but how much of it was true?

For the huge majority of people during Norman times everyday life hadn't changed that much from the pagan past, except for the newly-formed Christian rules imposed upon them. Most people were still working the land and scraping a living the best they could, with tradesmen beginning to specialise, and the concept of master craftsmen and city guilds emerging. The majority of people were extremely poor, partly due to the impossible taxes being levied to fund the lavish lifestyles of the few and the wars being fought by the reluctant many.

The darker side of this era, though, saw the introduction of foul methods of torture for crimes, with castle dungeons and village greens being the focus for such practices. Adulterers and bigamists were publicly humiliated or even tortured with the punishment being worse for women than men.

The now strongly established Catholic Christian church had it's own view on marriage, and new rules to go with it, which were also fear-driven and severely punishable should they be broken. This behaviour didn't last for long, and as Christianity evolved its temperance mellowed slightly for a while at least.

Marriage was taken more seriously as a result, however, and like most other arrangements between peoples everything had its price. Fines were now imposed upon anyone breaking Christian morality laws, which strengthened the subservience of lower classes and left the richer folks the only ones able to afford such luxuries. Higher on the list for peasant folk was the celebration of the eight annual festivals which marked the changes of the seasons and denoted the length of each day by the amount of sunlight in proportion to night time.

The majority of peoples alive at this time were poor farmers: everyone worked the land in some way or another, and these festivals coincided with the farming life cycle. They marked, lambing, ploughing, sowing, harvesting and culling amongst others.

The festival days were:

2 February / Imbolc / the start of spring
21 March / spring equinox / mid spring
1 May / Beltane / start of summer
21 June / summer solstice / mid-summer, days of equal length
1 August / Lammas / harvest / start of autumn
21 September / autumn equinox / mid autumn
1 November / Samhain / All Souls Day / new year
21 December / winter solstice / mid-winter / shortest day

These days we think of the year as linear, but for our pagan ancestors it was experienced as a cycle or circle. For those couples intending to reveal their love for each other to their community they could use the Beltane festival as an opportunity to seal their betrothal without it needing to cost anything.

If the community was already having a celebration or ritual to mark the fertile season then hand-fastings could be incorporated into this. For those who chose to keep it to themselves, they could perform their own private ritual and until such a time as they wished it to become public knowledge it would remain essentially their business. Lammas was also associated with marriage, and it's likely that either of these two fire festivals could have been used.

It is important to remember that throughout man's history there have always been two tiers of society—the rich and the poor. Up until Victorian times marriage was seen as a political and economic arrangement for the richer families to gain strength, but for the working classes it remained a simple affair based mainly on local customs.

2

Traditions

Medieval Celtic

The early Celtic/Catholic church records hand-fasting rituals where an already betrothed couple would go through a ceremony with symbolic remnants of the Druid influence, but inside a church, including the binding of the couple's left hands whilst vows are exchanged.

In parts of Ireland the left-hand practice is thought to have been recognition of a mistress rather than wife, so adding to the confusion. This was an early example of our modern pagan hand-fastings and probably the most closely related.

The ceremony would have included a priest, lawyer, scribe and the couple concerned, any others being optional. There would be incense, candles, water and some binding material, which varied depending on what the couple chose to use.

It is probable that vine or strips of green bark were used, but more recently recorded ceremonies used rope, hemp, twine, or ribbons, which are very popular today. The lawyer, probably an ovate or equivalent, would ensure that the couple could legally marry and warn them of the consequences should they be breaking any of the marriage laws. These moral laws still stand today as testament to our anciently held human values. The scribe would record the marriage although it was unlikely that anything remotely resembling a marriage certificate was issued—just a note in the newly kept parish records at most.

The priest would serve much the same role as today; in fact if you remove the actual hand-fastening or binding from the equation, twelfth-century ceremonies don't vary that much from modern ones.

Based on what little we know about medieval society, it is likely that betrothed couples marrying in church were of some status in their community. The joining of their offspring in a contractual marriage ensured security and protection for the families concerned. Marriage under these conditions was more about how well families got on with each other and what they could offer politically or financially than how much love the couple concerned actually felt for each other, but I like to believe this was considered. **It's interesting to observe our negative reactions in the western world to arranged marriages today, and yet they were almost definitely practised here until relatively recent times.**

Poorer tied labourers probably had more chance for romance than their richer counterparts. If you were already at the bottom of the social ladder you were bound, legally, to your Lord to stay there and marriages outside social groups were more uncommon. This isn't to say that they didn't happen. I'm sure they did but far less frequently and usually due to pregnancy, although that didn't always guarantee you a marriage. For the majority of people living menial and poverty-stricken lives on the land, simple hand-fastings were a distinct possibility.

It is a revelation to many that in most of Britain, almost up until the industrial revolution, a form of slavery was in operation, which made sure there were plenty of hands to work the land. These slaves, which probably accounted for a sizeable proportion of the population, didn't belong to anyone in the sense that we currently understand but were tied to their landowner. They offered him free labour and the promise of taking up arms for the king if needed, and in return were given protection—a very valuable commodity in those times—and land to grow food and keep their limited livestock on, which was not to be sniffed at. This began the tradition of tied cottages, which on many large country estates prevails to this day. Marriages within this class of people were simple, following local customs and traditions, and contained more of the old pagan elements than marriages higher up the social scale. To say that they bore any similarity to today's pagan rituals is stretching the imagination, but it is possible that there are some loose threads connecting back through time. The actual binding of hands, though, does seem to originate from medieval Scotland and Ireland, but as for elsewhere in England any definitive proof is sadly lacking.

Fires and Broomsticks

A tradition that is often associated with hand-fastings is jumping the fire. The newly married couple literally jump over a bonfire together for various reasons, one being to ensure continued passion throughout their marriage. It is impossible to pinpoint exactly when this custom started, but tales of such occasions abound in folklore and regional variations occur.

The Celtic Scots had, and in some cases still have, a tradition of burning a wicker man at Beltane and jumping the fire afterwards, which would ensure bravery, passion and fertility for the season. This tradition is usually practised on May Day by anyone brave enough, and is thought to be a part of celebrating the fire festival. It probably owes its origins to early drinking games, but the symbolism is nonetheless relevant.

Couples who had chosen this festival to marry would no doubt be encouraged to jump the fire together rather than individually, as they may have done in the past. They may have had a hand-fasting ritual before jumping the fire or they could announce their marriage as they did so, thus cementing it. Betrothal fire jumping is equally feasible, as it would indicate a leap of faith for the couple concerned in starting their journey of love and all its tests ahead. The fire could be symbolic of bravery where they were concerned.

Another jumping ceremony was celebrated in Wales, both in pre-Christian and modern times. This is known as 'jumping the broomstick'. There are two variations of this tradition: one includes the *priodas coes ysgub, priodas coes ysgubell,* otherwise known as the broomstick wedding.

Besom brooms made for such purposes used birch for love and oak for strength, which was great symbolically but had little practical use, the traditional besom being constructed from ash and birch.

One method included calling the oldest man of the village or community to witness the couple jumping the stick, which if carried out successfully would constitute a marriage. The other method was a little more complex and had the besom leaning in the doorway of the bride's house, broom head down. The couple were asked to jump the broom, groom first then bride. If either of the couple knocked it then the marriage was not recognised and it was seen as an omen for them to think again.

Interestingly no legal claims of ownership to property belonging to his bride could be made, but any children to this union were legitimate and would therefore inherit from both parents, so long as the couple remained married. If they wished to end the marriage, they had one year in which to change their minds; and as long as there were no children of the marriage during this time, they could annul it by simply asking the old man to return and witness them jumping back over the broom, in reverse this time, out of the house.

Irish Weddings

Irish weddings and their associated laws were similar to their Scottish cousins and came under the exclusively Irish *Brehon Law*. This very ancient law covered everything from the rights of kings and their successors to everyday subjects such as marriage. Any couple that produced children could consider themselves married and this would be recognised and upheld by the community with no stigma attached. Unlike English laws of the time, any property belonging to either party remained their own with no obligation to transfer ownership. Obviously in most cases they would cohabit, but neither of them could lay claim to each other's wealth.

Interestingly, many Irish weddings would be for a set period, often for twenty years (or until any children of the marriage grew up), which may well be the origins for our most common jointly held debt these days, the twenty-five year mortgage. Much like the rest of the British Isles the groom would pay a set price for his new bride, similar to a dowry, called a *Coibhce*, to the bride's father who, if feeling generous, would release this over time to the bride. When we think of it this makes perfect sense: instead of giving a lump sum to the father purely for his own use he could invest it wisely and help his daughter out as and when she needed it.

If the marriage were to break down then the groom would be expected to return to his family, taking with him any property he originally came with. Sometimes families would pay a commissary payment to whomever they felt deserved it. For example, if a wife committed adultery and her husband duly found out, he could leave the marriage and she may have to pay him back any monies given by her husband's family and vice versa. An Irish husband could in pre-Christian times take on as many wives as he could afford, something supported by the *Drom Ceat* meeting of 575 AD.

The Druid priesthood responsible for the spiritual and moral fibre of their community took the whole business very seriously. They were the intellectual mediators between people, expected to advise kings on the fairness of rule, and were extremely intelligent. These were days when marriage was definitely seen as a reason to rejoice, but a visit to your local knowledgeable one was expected before decisions were made. A couple would have to prove not only their love for each other but also their suitability and serious intent. A period of betrothal would be advised during which the couple could practise for the real thing. Although a precursor to modern day engagements, these betrothals included actually living as husband and wife.

If a child was born or expected by the couple during this time, then they would now be considered married and only the formality of a binding to declare this would now be expected. If on the other hand they changed their minds during this period, then provided they were still childless they could simply extract themselves from the engagement at the end of the year.

It is believed the Irish practised hand fastenings, so-called, as recognition of this betrothed year, and the wedding itself became the binding, so cementing the deal. Contracts were drawn up by both families and approved or otherwise by the local Druid order.

Saxon Weddings

Most of these weddings would be arranged. It is possible that the bride and groom had already met and may well have known each other fairly well through their families. Opportunities for them to get together would be provided by the families and hopefully they would like each other. It was an added bonus for the tribes if the couple could be guided into matrimony, as this gave the marriage a better start. The groom would have a modicum of say over his bride and could refuse her on the grounds of him finding her wholly unattractive. Any forced union such as this would be unproductive, to say the least.

People lived in smaller groups and had greater distances between them, so pressure for marriages was intense, causing many a headache for all those concerned.

Lower down the social scale marriage was based on the fertility of the mother of the bride: if she had borne several healthy strong babies then it followed that her daughter would too, and yet again we see women viewed much like cattle or other such domesticated animals.

Questions a prospective groom's father might ask were: 'Is she a good worker?', 'Is she from good healthy stock?', 'What does her father/tribe have to offer me?', 'Will this bond prove beneficial to my tribe?'—not very romantic but extremely relevant in those times.

During Saxon England everyone had their price or, as it was known then, *wergild.* Prospective wives had their own *wergild* and the larger this wedding payment was, the higher up the social scale the groom would be expected to be. A Kentish law of the time explains the effective power of *wergild* brilliantly: '*if any freeman lies with a freeman's wife let him pay for it with <u>her</u> wergild and provide for another wife out of his own money*'. That is, she would relinquish her property to her estranged husband as compensation, and her lover would have to pay for her keep from then on out of his money.

These were times when fines and compensation was the order of the day for any breach of moral or royal law—not unlike today really.

If, for example a man were to lay with a virgin slave of low order working for the royal household, he had to pay the price set then at about twelve shillings. This was an inordinate sum, quite outside the means of ordinary folk, so only rich men could afford to take such risks.

As non-payment of fines incurred greater punishments, usually of a vile and torturous kind, most often ending in death, people would pay up even if it meant starving or being reduced to outlaw status. Only fairly young fit men stood any chance of survival under these circumstances, but very few chose it as an alternative, knowing only too well how lonely, hungry, cold and fearful it would be for them.

King Alfred lay down some interesting laws regarding physical violation or attempts thereof. For a man to merely fondle the breast of any woman uninvited could cost him five shillings. To fully rape a freewoman would cost him sixty shillings, with all fines payable to the woman concerned.

Everything had its price and marriage was no exception. The marriage payment was determined through intense negotiation of the two fathers concerned and was called the *morgengifu* (of Viking origin), that simply means the morning gift payable by the husband the morning after the wedding night. This *gifu/gyfu* or gift went to the bride if she managed to maintain her virginity before marriage, hence the reason for giving it the morning after. This seems a little hard on girls, as we now know that it is perfectly feasible for women to break their hymen accidentally and proof of virginity does not always totally depend on this as a sign these days.

If the newly-married groom had reason to believe his wife was lying about her virginity it was up to him to decide which course to take. He could say nothing and the gift would duly arrive the next morning as expected, or he could choose to take umbrage with her and the marriage would be annulled and all gifts returned with her. Most Anglo-Saxons didn't worry too much about virginity unless his wife happened to be carrying another man's child, then it was a different matter and he could use the full force of the law against her.

The Saxons didn't mess about when it came to adultery. Any man found guilty of it would have to match his wife's *wergild* as compensation and her family could literally fight him to death if they so wished, but if he did die through such vengeance then that was an end to it and no further action on his family would be condoned.

Any woman found guilty of such an act would expect harsh treatment also: her husband could cast her out and keep her *wergild*. In Canute's time she could expect bloodier treatment and possibly lose her nose and ears. Ouch!

For the single young women of child-bearing age the pressure was on to comply with their family's wishes. Some could be as young as twelve and their grooms fourteen, although marriages of mixed ages, i.e. with large age gaps, were not uncommon.

Most girls hoped to be married by sixteen to eighteen years old and would often have strong ideas themselves as to prospective suitors. Often couples would meet and fall in love without any parental interference, but whether any marriage could come of this was a different matter. It was possible to approach their families and ask, the tradition being for the groom to try to impress his loved one's father, as continues to this day, and his chance of success lay in persuading the father that he was a good deal. If he could prove himself worthy, financially or otherwise, then he had some hope; but if the father concerned had a negative view of the marriage it was almost definitely doomed to failure.

Couples who dared to defy their parents would be risking alienation from their tribe and would find themselves being cast out of the society. This only ever happened in extreme circumstances and very rarely. They could start a life for themselves but unless they could find a village that would take them in then they were risking leading a harsh life alone, relying on their wits and ability to forage, and trying to avoid being victims of crime themselves. Life was hard enough and no one deliberately reduced themselves to begging unnecessarily. To be outcast from any group made it difficult to gain acceptance elsewhere and without that protection and security their chances of survival were slim.

Most young women were painfully aware of this and would do everything they could to attract the young man of their choice in the hope it would be an acceptable union in the eyes of their families. Some girls had to accept marriage to a suitor of greater years but many took this quite willingly as it assured them a secure place in society.

Going back to the legend of King Arthur, we see Guinevere being put in exactly this position despite her feelings for Lancelot. As in this story, many affairs and indiscretions occurred and sometimes it resulted in the creation of illegitimate heirs. Marriage was probably a far more complex issue then than it is today, with many disputed titles and lineages.

Marriage for those farther up the social scale followed a similar path but more emphasis was placed on political and military gains, and this set the scene until relatively recently. If a marriage joined two previously separate tribes then they would be expected to have greater strength in battle with the amalgamation and more political clout regionally. Marriages were often arranged between the leaders of such groups purely for these gains. Again, love came very low down on the list of priorities for the couple concerned. The actual ceremony, however, would have been as grand an affair as the bride's family could provide, a tradition continued to this day with many people. If the wedding were of high status then a public holiday would be announced with everyone joining in the celebration.

There would be the formalities of the ceremony itself, many of which depended on the local customs, followed by feasting and drinking with entertainment laid on. Gifts would be exchanged, as would any payment for the bride herself. The ceremony would be a religious affair, most probably held in the open air but within the enclave of the settlement, weather permitting, or inside if the groom's abode lent itself to such an occasion.

Early Christian churches were being built by Saxon times and if converted the couple may have used one for their wedding. If they still followed the old ways then a priest would officiate and call upon whichever fertility god or goddess the families still worshipped to recognise and bless the union, with the emphasis being placed on the future fertility of the impending union.

It is also interesting to note at this point that the responsibility of fertility rested with the woman until relatively recently and to be barren was seen as a very bad omen, possibly indicating some evilness of the female's doing. It was dangerous to be found infertile and male infertility was *not* recognised.

Other members of his or her order would be present to protect, record and oversee the legal implications of the marriage. Various methods of protection were used to deter any evil or malevolent forces, including appropriate chanting, incenses and herbs. The couple would exchange vows whilst holding hands, which could possibly be bound symbolically, but we have no real evidence of this, as I have said, until later times. The throwing of grain over the newly-weds after the ceremony originates from this period. Again, this was to help ensure their fertility and general good fortune.

An interesting tradition that continued up until 1929, but had its roots in Saxon times, was the practice of selling the wife on if she did not come up to scratch. This may have been a blessing or a tragedy to the wife depending on the circumstances.

Tudor Weddings

By now the Catholic church was very much in control of most of the British Isles and the contractual or binding marriage ceremony was completely established. Very few people still worshipped in the old way or practised any magical arts except for medicinal herbcraft, which was still tolerated for obvious reasons.

As part of the groom's payment, the giving of a ring to the bride had been introduced and a popular innovation was the Gimmal ring resurrected from an earlier Roman tradition. This ring was in fact three rings that interlocked and represented the Holy Trinity. The first part was given upon the couple's betrothal, the second presented on the day of the actual wedding ceremony, and the third on arrival of the first child. The significance of this particular finger owes its origins to the Romans, who believed that an artery led from there directly to the heart.

The wedding cake, traditionally a simnel cake, had also been around since Roman times, but it is believed that the Tudors dropped the previous tradition of breaking the cake over the couple's heads for the more sensible practice of sharing it among the guests.

In some parts of the British Isles, predominantly Scotland, Ireland, Wales and Cornwall, where many of the indigenous Celtic peoples still survived, the physical binding of hands has been recorded as still occurring in Tudor times. The wedding ceremony now took place inside a church or cathedral, depending on the couple's status, and was carried out by a priest in Latin.

Despite many laws being placed on marriage, both the ancient pagan ones and subsequent Christian ones remained optional for the common people. The Tudors changed all this by introducing the concept of legality where children were concerned. Considering the phenomenal implications of proving patriarchy until then it is amazing it took us this long to do something about it. The introduction of the Trent Council Act of 1537 made it a legal requirement to be married by clergy in a consecrated church. Children born out of Christian wedlock were for the first time considered illegitimate, and the seeds of the 'shotgun' marriage were sown. An illegitimate child could not take its father's name or inherit from either parent, and a stigma built up because of this.

An official service had to be introduced that would lay the foundations of today's ceremonies. All the legally recognised marriages in England now took place exclusively in a church. The symbolism of the four elements were still represented and in some areas after the service the couple were often required to circle the altar three times deosil (clockwise). The couple would be expected to face each other at the end of the ceremony and the giving of a ring replaced the practice of hand fastening or holding.

Fathers were now expected to give their daughters away whereas previously they gave themselves away by consent. Although becoming a complicated affair, the ancient morality laws still stood regarding marriage and one famous historical figure that came up against these laws was Henry VIII. His first wife, Catherine of Aragon, was older than he and although she gave him a daughter, Mary, she was considered unlikely to be able to produce any more children.

This left Henry in a predicament: he wanted a male heir and had fallen in love with a lady-in-waiting, Anne Boleyn. To obtain a divorce was difficult and required papal permission, which was rarely ever given. Henry tried to prove the illegitimacy of the union by claiming he'd already broken a Catholic law by marrying his dead father's wife, but the Pope of the time did not concur. Henry took drastic measures and began the now famous reformation and dissolution of the monasteries instigating the complete pillage and breakdown of power within the Catholic church in England.

Setting himself up as the newly appointed head of the Protestant Church of England, he set about radically changing the marriage laws to suit. It worked as far as his divorce and subsequent marriage was concerned, but started a war with Rome and other Catholic nations.

Another Tudor figure who caused a furore over her decisions regarding marriage was Henry's daughter Elizabeth. Once on the throne, pressure to marry was her biggest problem and one she resisted at all costs. To Elizabeth, who had experienced her mother's execution due to her father's radical reforms on marriage and divorce, it represented a fearful act that could result in death. Having had her own heart broken by a man who lied about his married status didn't help either, so she managed to avoid it even though she was under extreme pressure to do otherwise by her privy council. Marriage by now had become an institution and one that had the severest penalties for indiscretions or breaking of its laws—even execution! But we do have Henry to thank for re-introducing legal divorces.

Traditional Legacies

Let's look at what has survived from days of old regarding wedding ceremonies and superstitions.

1. Hand-fastings, bindings, tying the knot and the exchange of rings are all thought to have evolved from pagan times, with actual hand holding or binding being the most probable common denominator.
2. Laws regarding incest, bigamy, age, barrenness and impotence being reasons for divorce or annulment.
3. Representation of the four elements, earth (gifts, dowry), air (vows exchanged), fire (either to leap over or candles) and water or wine (sometimes sprinkled over the couple).
4. A priest or official and witnesses as in today's ceremonies, whether church or registry office.
5. Symbols of fertility—appropriate flowers, herbs, cake and grain or more recently confetti.
6. Stag nights and hen nights thought to originate from Greece.
7. A period of betrothal before marriage.
8. Gifts exchanged replacing dowries.
9. Wedding feast.

3

Modern Hand-fastings

The most important fact to digest about a pagan wedding is that, in the eyes of today's society and the laws put upon it, **it is NOT legal** in the British Isles, which is worth remembering. There are some States in America that do recognise pagan marriages but unless you happen to live there it's a nice to know rather than a need to know; but for those of you hand-fasting over the water *Hand-Fasted and Heart Joined* by Lady Maeve Rhea provides an excellent list and is included in the bibliography. Some couples like to have a certificate drawn up to sign, but it will not be recognised officially.

The examples of such certificates I have seen are usually either computer designed by the couple for the occasion and signed on the day by the priest/priestess, or scribed by hand which is nice if you are, or know of, a skilled calligrapher.

If you wish to be thought of as legally husband and wife, in this country, today you have the same two options as the rest of us, and that is church or civil service. It surprises most people to learn that although these take several elements from the ancient past, it is impossible to define how accurate they are to weddings held BCE. The practice of these ceremonies has come about during the past century due to the revival of interest in all things pagan. Actually openly holding such a ritual is even younger and thought to be post Gardnerian (Gerald Gardner, founder of modern Wicca at some time between 1930 and 1950), or about fifty years old, which coincides with the repeal of the Witch Craft Act of 1951.

Certificate

of

Hand-Fasting

Celebrated this day of May 1st

The love and pledged lifetime commitment
of love between

Gavin Bruce & Dianne Brown

Witnessed by

....

(witness)

....

(witness)

and bound together in love and honour
of the God & Goddess
by

....

(priest/priestess)

Love binds us
Love strengthens us
Love is our creed
Blessed Be

This is a basic example just to give you an idea of what can be achieved.

Interestingly this does not apply in Scotland as you can still be tried for 'acts' of witchcraft there. They vary considerably depending upon the region in which they are held, local traditions and those the couple follow. The majority fall into one of these groups: Celtic, Norse, Anglo-Saxon and more recently Wicca, in these Isles anyway.

Looking back on the common traditional legacies as mentioned in chapter 2, we find that most of these are covered by today's hand-fastings. It's interesting to see that, of all the recorded history of marriage, the binding of hands remains the most elusive to prove and yet the most popular part of modern ceremonies.

Most modern pagans prefer to hold their marriage out of doors and are quite particular about where they marry. If choosing to hold your ceremony on common ground do not automatically assume you can without checking with the local council concerned for any by-laws that may prevent you from doing so. Similarly if you wish to use any National Trust land or land belonging to any conservation group it is best to ask first or risk having your day ruined by objectors. Many modern pagans use a garden, whether their own or someone else's, and that's possibly the safest option.

Who you choose to officiate at your wedding will depend on a number of factors, one being the tradition you belong to and its current policy on hand-fastings, another being personal preference for a particular initiated priest or priestess (some require one of each), and lastly if you are eclectic or solitary then you can use whomever you want, really initiated or otherwise.

Just like our pagan ancestors, modern practitioners of the craft are relaxed and open minded in their attitude to marriage ritual and ceremony. Some modern traditions are developing guidelines for rites of passage and Wicca is one such example.

Wiccan Hand-fastings

A Wiccan couple wishing to be wed today are given several options. One is to hand-fast for a year (and a day if they wish) and then decide whether to renew their vows for life. This kind of betrothal/trial marriage is probably a very good idea, especially for the younger pagans or those who have not been married before.

Some couples decide on a set number of years, which I personally find rather strange. It's like saying I'll love you for *x* years, no more no less. They can of course extend this option if they require. Some opt for saying 'as long as love survives' which is honest and realistic at least. The most popular hand-fasting is intended for life, theoretically, but it shows the couple are committed and devoted to one another.

The bravest of souls decide to hand-fast for eternity, not something to be entered into lightly I feel. Once you decide which period of marriage to opt for then approach an initiated priest or priestess; some branches of Wicca prefer both to be in attendance. The priest/priestess will then ask the couple a number of questions about how they want their day to go. The most important factors are:

1. Why do you want a Wiccan marriage?
2. Where do you want to hold the ceremony?
3. When do you plan to have it?
4. What sort of ceremony do you want?
5. Who do you wish to attend?

These questions are very important and give both the couple and the priest/priestess a chance to get to know one another if they don't already.

The answer to the first question decides whether the couple really know what is meant by Wicca—an important consideration for both parties—and you would be amazed at how many people have just heard a little about it but don't really understand the depth of spirituality involved, which can put some couples off!

The second question will need to be looked into for its feasibility. You'd be surprised at some of the places people want to be hand-fasted these days!

The third is important from both a religious and a weather perspective. Some days are better than others and some times of year too, another consideration some couples don't seem to have gone into!

Beltane (1 May) or Lammas (1 August) are by far the most popular dates, and days chosen between these dates would be considered auspicious. Due to their popularity they are booked up quickly, so get in early to avoid disappointment. Choosing a day on either a waxing or full moon would be advisable, as waning and dark phases are probably better for separation or divorce rather than marriage. Mid-day is ideal, and likely to be the most convenient time for your guests, with dawn OK for betrothals and sunsets good for older couples or second timers.

This is not to say that you cannot consider alternative times of year and for any couple who especially love autumn then fine, go ahead, but think about the moon's phase and avoid Samhain, 31 October, altogether for obvious reasons.

Next, do you want an informal or formal hand-fasting? This is very important to agree on, as the priest/priestess will need to know how many other people could be needed officially for the ceremony.

Finally, the fifth question is important, as you must consider your guests and their comfort throughout the day.

Once all these formalities are decided then you are set on the road to your hand-fasting. On the day of the marriage some couples still follow some of the more modern superstitions regarding marriage, and brides for example could be wearing something old, something new, something borrowed, something blue, etc. Grooms might not have been allowed to see their bride the day before the marriage.

How you arrive at the venue is up to you, and many different ways can be found. A horse and carriage is popular, and walking also if one is close enough, such as in your garden. Once assembled the priest/priestess will cast two circles, one the inner sanctum, which may contain an altar, and an outer circle for guests and other officiates if present. Not all Wiccans cast two circles and it is not strictly necessary.

The circumference of the outer circle is largely dictated by the size of the group, but the inner one is usually nine or twelve feet in diameter.

What the couple wear is completely up to them, although placing some symbolism can strengthen the magic of the day. If a couple decides to marry at Beltane then they may like to wear green and appropriate spring flowers like hawthorn and crab apple blossom, which has the added bonus of smelling delicious. They can choose their own binding material and many nowadays opt for stripped bark or ribbons, which can be very colourful and also significant.

Rose is the flower most associated with marriage—it represents the beauty of the bride combined with the strength and virility of the groom. For our more eternal friends, lilies are a good choice, being symbolic of re-birth originally—not death as more commonly believed.

The priest/priestess will have already discovered the direction of north and the wedding entourage will be asked to orient themselves accordingly to the four quarters or 'directions' of north, south, east and west. Once happily assembled the priest/priestess will ask his or her helpers, if there are any, to call in the directions or quarters. This is simply asking for the spirits of the north (earth), east (air), south (fire) and west (water), to be present and bless the couple. Just in case you need guidance in this it can be done as follows:

North: *I call upon the spirits of the north, of earth, the rock of ages, from which our needs are met, that contains all knowledge and bears testament to our deeds upon it to be here and energise this binding of love today.*

East: *I call upon the spirits of the east, of air, our life breath, the inspiration, from which words flow, make them only of love and energise this special day.*

South, *I call upon the spirits of the south, of fire, the energy and passion rise within your flame, let the sun shine down on us and energise this special day.*

West: *I call upon the spirits of the west, of water, that allows the movement of love and healing for all living things, let the moon's tide energise our love today.*

Then the goddess and her consort the god are called, during which the guests, if any are present, are normally holding hands to contain the energy raised and add to it. There are several ways in which Wiccan's approach the calling of these two primal forces from simply

'I call upon the energy of the Goddess to be here and bless this couple, I call upon the energy of the God to be here and bless this couple'
to longer and more formal callings

'Oh great mother, Goddess, I call you in the name of .... and .... to be here in our sacred circle cast in your honour to bless this loving couple on this day of joy and happiness. May your love flow through them in their life together and enrich every moment that they are together and give them strength for any times apart. Share with them your beauty, gentleness, wisdom and healing that they may grow closer together. Protect them from any that wish them harm and banish the influence of those who do so. Let your light and love become part of their journey together and may it shine on others in their midst.

The bride can now give her goddess gift to her groom saying something along the lines of
This symbol of the goddess within me is yours to keep as is my heart and soul, to your body I will remain faithful, and your honour I will defend.

The groom accepts the gift and now the priest/priestess calls in the god

Oh great father our god, I call you in the name of .... and .... to be present here in this circle cast in honour of the goddess and you her god, bless this loving couple on this day of love and happiness. May your love flow through them and fertilise their union sealing their fate together as one. Share with them your strength, enthusiasm, wildness and knowledge that they may build a secure future. Let your love and light shine down on their path ahead.

The groom now gives his bride a god gift saying, for example,

This symbol of the god within me is yours to keep, as is my heart and soul, to your body I will remain faithful, and your honour I will defend.

This is a powerful part of the ceremony and can be overwhelming for those who have not experienced it before, so I feel it helps if the priest/priestess explains all this beforehand.

The couple then stand facing each other as the official asks them to declare their personal pre-written intentions and love for each other, an example of which can be seen at the start of the book. After this the priest/priestess asks them to join their left hands and winds the binding material around their wrists.

This is usually done in one of two ways, the first being that the couple take hold of each other's arms just above the wrist, allowing the priest/priestess to bind around the outside of both wrists three times, once for the goddess, once for the god, and once for their love. Any words spoken during this part of the ritual are done so by the priest/priestess and may go along the lines of

Now you have declared your love for each other in the presence of the Goddess and God and these witnesses here present I fasten you, once for the Goddess, once for the God and once for your spirits which are now bound as one.

The second method is mainly for couples who wish to become fastened for life or eternity and involves the cord being threaded between the couple's hands in a figure of eight. The rest is pretty much the same with the exception being that the priest/priestess declares their intent for life or for ever.

The couple are now blessed by the elements which should be to hand, which is why it's nice to organise a pretty wedding altar in advance. This is achieved by the priest/priestess holding out either a bowl of earth or crystal for the couple's bound hands to touch, then incense or feathers representing air (blowing on the couple's hands is also acceptable), letting a candle or suitable flame very lightly skim their hands (this is potentially dangerous so be sensible, and if worried just hold it near them—you don't want them to catch fire!), and lastly a bowl or chalice of pre-blessed purified water for them to dunk their fingers in, or you can sprinkle some over them. Natural spring water is best.

The married couple must thank the goddess and the god and bid them farewell, then treat the elements with the same respect. This is normally done thus:

Priest/priestess: *We give our love, light and thanks to the Goddess for blessing us with your presence and bid you farewell. We give our love, light and thanks to the God for blessing us with your presence and bid you farewell.*

(It is often a good idea to practise this with the couple beforehand so they can say it with you.)

North: *We give love, light and thanks to the spirits of the North for blessing us with your energy and bid you farewell.*

East: *We give love, light and thanks to the spirits of the East for blessing us with your energy and bid you farewell.*

South: *We give love, light and thanks to the spirits of the South for blessing us with your energy and bid you farewell.*

West: *We give love, light and thanks to the spirits of the West for blessing us with your energy and bid you farewell.*

There are endless permutations of this ritual, and it must be stressed that all this book is setting out to achieve is guidance and at the end of the day it will be down to the couple concerned to decide, with help from a priest or priestess, what is best for them. The emphasis is usually on creating a special magical and deeply spiritual day unique to that couple, not a fancy dress competition or hours of ritual that reduces your guests to tears of boredom and despair. I would advise you to keep it to about half an hour at most, as any longer can result in aching limbs, full bladders and very hungry folk put off hand-fastings for ever.

Going back to the gifts exchanged between the couple during the ceremony, these can be whatever you wish but many couples like to use something spiritually significant.

A groom could give his bride an acorn, promising her strength and a love that will endure. The bride could give her groom a lock of her hair as a token of trust and a keepsake for when they are apart. The ideas are limitless, and it's very much up to personal preference in the end.

If the couple have decided on any broomstick or fire jumping, now is a good time to do it. Some couples like to ask guests to bring offerings, which can be an alternative to wedding presents. Now they are married and all that is left is to thank the official who may have given of his or her time freely, and party!

Variations occur throughout the Wiccan world, which like most paths is constantly evolving and adapting to the modern world. Some Wiccan ceremonies can be much humbler affairs but set somewhere so beautiful that they frequently feel the most magical.

It must be noted that many priestesses and priests give of their time without expecting payment, but to offer travelling expenses, a gift or gratuity and a free feed would be very much appreciated by many. The matter of fixed payment for services rendered amongst the pagan community is hotly disputed and one feels we may have to all agree to disagree over this subject. Personally I feel that if some priests and priestesses are more popular than others, either by self election or otherwise, one cannot expect them to give up their valuable time free and gratis, but at the end of the day it is up to the couple concerned whether they want to pay or not. Some will do it for free and others not but we should not judge their suitability on this alone. If in doubt, leave that one out, is my advice. Personal recommendation is probably the best reason for your choice.

Eclectic Hand-fastings

Many of today's practising pagans are eclectic, drawing energy from two or more traditions and their deities. Purists would possibly frown on this, but it has to be remembered that all paths ultimately grew from the same seed and more or less reach for the same goal. I feel the key to travelling several paths at once is to blend that which they have in common without mixing deities or symbols thereof. For anyone considering calling on a mixed family—beware, just like us mere mortals they don't always get on!

It is, however, perfectly possible to mix various wedding traditions such as jumping the broomstick, decorations of woodland foliage, wedding favours, binding of hands, fire jumping, etc., without upsetting the natural order of things or jeopardising your day in any way. It is also possible to hold a pagan hand-fasting without it being overtly pagan. For some of you on an eclectic path, the following order of service is superb, managing to include several traditional practices and expressing the couple's spiritual message without the need for any high ritual. If you are of mixed paths within the relationship, this type of service might suit both parties and is unlikely to cause offence to any other religious denominations present.

We are invited to look back at Mandy and Donald's hand-fasting, held on 21 June 2002 inside a beautiful ancient tithe barn deep in the Northamptonshire countryside, England. Inside their families and friends are already gathered, sitting on rows of rustic benches, able to admire the heavily laden beams draped with garlands of leaves and flowers above them and also the flickering flames of the many candles. Their bridesmaids, who will also play the role of elementals during the service, hold four pretty posies, having been positioned correctly in the quarters aligned with an eastern altar. Across the inside of the arched oak doors lies a broomstick, which the couple will cross before making their way past the facing aisles of their expectant audience. The priestess and her assistant 'readers' await their arrival in front of the altar with its grand church candles burning brightly, creating a focal point for all.

As we join them Fourwillow (one of four readers) opens the ceremony

Fourwillow: *The broomstick or besom is traditionally used to sweep away negativity from the home, and heart. Jumping the broomstick signifies the effort a couple must share, leaving their single, separate lives behind them, united in their new life together. They must be there for each other to give a steadying hand, to guide each other forward. The broom symbolises the hurdles they must face. If they do not jump together they will stumble. Once bonded, the broom will be used to sweep away their past lives, so they may start afresh, making way for a long and harmonious life together.*

(Open doors, Ronald & Mandy stand in the entrance.)

Fourwillow: *Do you Ronald and Mandy enter here today, leaving the past at the door?*

Couple: *We do.*

Fourwillow: *Are you ready to make your first journey together?*

Couple: *We are.*

Fourwillow: *Then you are invited to jump the broomstick.*

(Couple jump the broomstick and walk down the aisle.)

Oakilia: *We stand upon this holy earth and in the face of heaven to witness the sacred rite of marriage between Ronald and Mandy. Just as we come together as family and friends so we ask for the Greater powers to be present here within our Circle. May this sacred union be filled with their holy presence, no matter what your own personal beliefs.*

Fourwillow: *The joining together of man and woman in the sacred Rite of Marriage brings together great forces from which may flow the seeds of future generations to be nurtured within the walls of time. Within every masculine nature lies the feminine, within every*

feminine nature lies the masculine. The interplay of masculine and feminine forces when flowing freely in a union based upon true love finds many expressions. The union is truly holy.

Reader one reads, 'The Dance'

A good relationship has a pattern like a dance, and is built on some of the same rules. The partners do not need to hold on tightly, because they move confidently in the same pattern, intricate but gay, and swift and free, like a country-dance by Mozart. To touch heavily would be to arrest the pattern and freeze the movement, to check the endlessly changing beauty of its unfolding. There is no place here for the possessive clutch, the clinging arm, the heavy hand; only the barest touch in passing. Now arm in arm, now face to face, now back to back—it does not matter which, because they know they are partners moving to the same rhythm, creating a pattern together, and being invisibly nourished by it.

The joy of such a pattern is not only the joy of creation or the joy of partnership, it is also the joy of living in the moment. Lightness of touch and living in the moment are intertwined.

Oakilia: *Who walks the path of the moon to stand before heaven and declare her sacred vows?*

(The woman to be married steps forward)

Mandy: *I do.*

Fourwillow: *Who walks the path of the sun to stand upon this holy earth and declare his sacred vows?*

(The man to be married steps forward)

Fourwillow: *Do you Ronald come to this place of your own free will?*

Ronald: *I do.*

(Both must walk the symbolic paths of the sun and moon, clockwise and anticlockwise returning to the eastern gate)

Oakilia: *Ronald and Mandy, you have walked the symbolic paths of the Sun and Moon. Will you now walk together the circle of time, travelling through the elements and the seasons?*

Couple: *We will.*

(Both walk to the northern gate.)

North: *Will your love survive the times of stillness and restriction?*

Couple: *It will.*

North: *Then accept the blessing of the Element of Earth in this the place of winter. May your union be strong and fruitful.*

(Both walk to the eastern gate)

East: *Will your love survive the clear light of day?*

Couple: *It will.*

East: *Then accept the blessing of the Element of Air in this the place of spring. May your marriage be blessed by the light of every new dawn.*

(Both walk, holding hands, to the southern gate.)

South: *Will your love survive the harsh fires of change?*

Couple: *It will.*

South: *Then accept the blessing of the Element of Fire in this the place of summer. May your home be filled with warmth.*

(Both walk to the western gate.)

West: *Will your love survive the ebb and flow of feeling?*

Couple: *It will.*

Fourwillow: *All things in Nature are circular—night becomes day, day becomes night and night becomes day again. The moon waxes and wanes and waxes again. There is Spring, Summer, Autumn, Winter and Spring again. These things are part of the great mysteries.*

Oakilia: *Who is the keeper of the rings?*

(The keeper of the rings comes forward with the ceremonial cushion.)

Ring Bearer: *I am.*

Oakilia: *Then before all present repeat these words.*

Woman: (facing the man in order to give him the ring): *Accept in freedom this circle of gold as a token of my vows. With it I pledge my love, my strength, my friendship. I will honour you, respect and cherish you, I bring you joy now and forever.*

Man: (Facing the woman and giving her a ring) *Accept in freedom this circle of gold as a token of my vows. With it I pledge my love, my strength, my friendship. I will honour you, respect and cherish you. I bring you joy now and forever.*

Woman: *In the name of the Goddess I bring to you the warmth of my heart.*

(Her first woman brings her a lit taper)

Man: *In the name of the God of love I bring you the light of my love.*

(His first man hands him a lit taper.)
(Both light a single candle in the centre.)

Reader Two reads a Native American poem

May the Sun bring you new strength by day,
May the Moon softly restore you by night,
May the rain-wash away your fears,
And the breeze invigorate your being.

May you, all the days of your life,
Walk gently through the world,
And know its beauty.

Now you will feel no rain, for each will shelter the other.
Now you will feel no cold, for each will warm the other.
Now you will feel no solitude, for each will company the other.

Now you are two persons, but both will lead one life.
Go now to your dwelling to begin the days of your life together.
And may the days be good and long upon the Earth.

(Oakilia ties the hands of the couple)

Fourwillow: '*Tying the knot' is a term we have inherited to describe*
the marriage of a man to a woman, but its roots can be found in the
old pagan tradition of hand-fasting, symbolising the joining of two as
one. People holding hands with each other is in itself a sign of unity,
but hand-fasting shows that a mutual bond of mutual love and
commitment is being made, each to each other.

Hymn. Lord of the Dance, verse by the singers. All sing the
chorus

Dance then wherever you may be,
I am the Lord of the Dance said he,
And I'll lead you all wherever you may be,
And I'll lead you all in the dance said he.

All: *May the warmth and love of your union be blessed.*

(Hands are untied)

Oakilia: *Do you swear upon the sword of justice to keep sacred your*
vows?

Couple: *We swear.*

Fourwillow: *Then seal your promise with a kiss.*

(The couple kiss)

Fourwillow: *Beneficial spirits and the souls of our ancestors accept the*
union of your children. Help them, guide them, protect and bless
their home and the children born of their union. May they work
together in times of ease and times of hardship, knowing that they
are truly blessed. From this time forth you walk together along
life's path, may your way be blessed.

51

Reader Three reads the Celtic Blessing

Goodness of the sea be yours,
Goodness of the earth be yours,
Goodness of heaven.

Each day be joyous to you,
No day be grievous to you,
Love of each face be yours.

A bright flame before thee,
A guiding star above thee,
A smooth path below thee,

Today, tonight, and forever more.

Oakilia thanks the four directions

Elemental East, we thank thee
For giving us inspiration,
And as we bid you fond farewell,
Give freedom to imagination.

Elemental South, we thank thee,
For giving us courage and passion,
And as we bid you fond farewell,
Our hearts take flight in rhythm.

Elemental West, we thank thee,
For giving us compassion and love,
And as we bid you fond farewell,
Rain peace on Earth from above.

Elemental Earth, we thank thee,
For keeping us safe and secure,
And as we bid you fond farewell,
Prosper forever more.

(The participants are instructed to make the three circles of existence. The couple hold hands to make a circle within a circle. Participants in the seated horseshoe then join hands to form a third circle.)

All:
We swear by peace and love to stand
Heart to heart and hand in hand
Mark o spirit and hear us now
Confirming this our sacred vow.

Fourwillow: *This sacred rite of marriage ends in peace as in peace it began. Let us withdraw, holding peace and love in our hearts until we meet again.*

Oakilia directs the bridesmaids

Bridesmaids leave, scattering flowers for the happy couple to walk on and to go and begin their new life together. Everyone leaves, escorted by bridesmaids. Confetti may be thrown outside the barn.

This example of a modern hand-fasting was kindly lent to me by Oakilia, a self-initiated goddess-oriented solitary practitioner of 'The Craft' with over 25 years' experience, who resides in the beautiful Cambridgeshire countryside and is an often sought out performer of hand-fastings in her area. Whilst visiting Oakilia's lovely home she agreed to answer some of the most commonly asked questions people normally have on hand-fasting.

MN: How long have you been performing hand-fastings?

Oakilia: For about the last three seasons.

MN: Have you ever had to turn anyone down?

Oakilia: No.

MN: Would you?

Oakilia: Yes.

MN: For what reasons?

Oakilia: If I had doubts I would advise the couple to have a tarot reading to look at their suitability. This is because I have complete trust in my readings, and if the result were negative I would trust the guidance and encourage them to think again.

MN: What types of hand-fasting ceremonies can you hold for people?

Oakilia: I can adapt to pretty much any path as long as it is not a dark one.

MN: Would you object to a skyclad ceremony?

Oakilia: No, not necessarily, as long as *everyone* was skyclad, although this is highly unlikely these days.

MN: How long in advance do you recommend couples to plan ahead for?

Oakilia: At least six months, ideally.

MN: How many meetings would be required prior to the event?

Oakilia: It depends on how complicated an event they are planning really, several.

MN: Would you have any problems calling on deities you are not familiar with?

Oakilia: No, I would familiarise myself with them and call on them for guidance well beforehand.

MN: If a couple approached you determined to include some sort of pre-celebration sacrifice, how would you advise them?

Oakilia: I would advise a symbolic one only. I would never allow any life to be spent or blood to be spilt at one of my ceremonies.

MN: Are there any specific times of the year you avoid holding hand-fastings?

Oakilia: Yes, I avoid from 31 October until the end of April, as is traditional, and choose the most auspicious day and moon cycle.

MN: This next subject seems to be a bone of contention amongst the pagan community, but, do you think we should be charging for these rites of passage?

Oakilia: Yes, I believe that anyone giving of their time and expertise should receive a fair payment in return. We charge for goods and readings why not rites?

MN: Finally, when carrying out the ritual do you use your own tools?

Oakilia: Yes, I always use my own tools. It's more reliable and I wouldn't want to mess with any one else's.

MN: Thank you for giving of your time so freely today Oakilia, and blessings.

Oakilia: It was a pleasure.

The next person I was lucky enough to interview was Kathy Jones, Priestess of Avalon in the spiritual heart of England, Glastonbury. Kathy is a very highly sought after priestess for rites of passage including hand-fastings and has been performing them for fifteen years now. Most of her ceremonies are held in the magical garden of the Chalice Well, a unique and deeply sacred site. I asked her about the types of service she offers and she informed me that like most people in the pagan community she could be flexible. Her only prerequisite was that any couple approaching her must want a spiritual day, as her main role is to invoke divine energy to bless the couple.

She has her own individual method for performing the actual binding that is carried out at the end of the ceremony. This requires the female to bring a hoop symbolic of the goddess and the male a wand symbolic of the god. The complicated binding of the couple's hands with the hoop and wand results in the couple then being able to remove their hands at the end, leaving the wand and hoop still joined, which they take home and keep thus until such a time, if indeed there is one, that they unbind or choose to renew their vows.

Kathy places great emphasis on the careful selection of these vows and reminds her clientele to be very thoughtful in their

Marriage Blessing Ceremony & Celtic Hand-fasting

Programme

Calling of directions, Elements, Goddesses and Gods

With invocation of the Divine by ceremonialist

Cleansing by Air and Incense

Cleansing of participants with incense

Telling the tale of how you first met

Purification by Fire

Encircling you with candle flame, the light of inspiration

Confession of love to each other

Blessing by Water

Sharing a chalice of Holy spring waters

Exchange of Solemn vows (to be written by participants)

Exchange of rings

Blessing by Earth and Celtic hand-fasting

Joining hands, hoop and wand, with ribbons,
The loving ties which bind us together

Closing Blessing

Closing of Directions

It is with gratitude and thanks to Kathy Jones that we have this programme, which she produces for couples who inquire about her services.

choice of words. Words have power in themselves and even more so in front of divine witnesses. In theory Kathy is happy to call on most traditional deities but will offer guidance on sensible and/or personally appropriate energetic beings.

I asked her for her opinion on the ethics of charging for services and, like Oakilia and myself, among many others, she said she doesn't feel it's unethical to charge for her time. It is valuable, as is her own particular expertise. I agreed with Kathy mainly on principle but also for the sake of common-sense.

Kathy is used to the energy of the place in which she holds her hand-fastings, and is an experienced priestess, making her better placed than some to do the best for any couple she hand-fasts.

Druid Ceremonies Irish and Scottish Celtic Traditions

Modern Druid hand-fasting ceremonies don't vary that much from their Wiccan counterparts in format. If you are on a Celtic path and intend to hold a hand-fasting, then approaching a Druid priest or priestess is the first step. It's possible that you already know one, but if not then contact either the Pagan Federation or the Order of Bards and Ovates—addresses for both are at the end of the book. Hand-fastings of this kind are almost exclusively held outside, most often in an ancient grove or similar. If the weather is abysmal then you can go inside but it's a good idea to take plenty of foliage with you. Druid means *of the trees* and therefore trees are an integral part of any Druid path. Most Druid hand-fastings will have both a priest and priestess in attendance and specific deities will be invoked through them during the ceremony. Depending on how true to ancient paths you wish to be, a contract can be drawn up beforehand and witnessed on the day by anyone you trust to do this, usually a friend or friends—it's up to you. For those wanting guidance on writing contracts here is a very simplified example.

Hand-fasting Contract

I (bride) the undersigned promise to take seriously this day of

....

My hand-fasting to (groom).

With the blessing and approval of my family I will from this day on recognise him as my husband.

To our marriage I bring all my worldly goods and will commit all my income to the betterment of the union.

These goods and monies will remain my property throughout.

If at any point our marriage dissolves I will claim rights to these properties and half of any accrued in the interim.

With the exception of my horse Dobbin.

I (groom) the undersigned promise to take seriously this day of

....

My hand-fasting to (bride).

With the blessing and approval of my family I will from this day on recognise her as my wife.

To my marriage I bring all my worldly goods and will commit all my income to the betterment of the union.

These goods and properties will remain my property throughout.

If at any point our marriage dissolves I will claim rights to these properties and any accrued in the interim.

With the exception of my vintage Ford.

Signed (bride)...

Signed (groom) ....

Witness (bride's witness)..

Witness (groom's witness) ....

Date ....

Ok, so I've trivialised a little, but you get the idea.

The above contract bears a strong resemblance to a modern pre-nuptial agreement in very basic form. The idea is to set out the financial arrangements of the marriage and any debating about sharing future costs, etc., can be sorted at this point. Speaking to many divorcees on this issue I found that most would opt for some sort of pre-wedding agreement, as most have experienced money problems and differing ideas on roles they were expected to play within the marriage. Some couples have incredibly long-winded contracts, going into the smallest of details, but you can make it as simple or as complicated as you feel you need, if at all! As already mentioned the marriage contract is optional, but for our forebears it contained all the relevant information required to protect the individual's property, and it helped to know how many sheep you started out with! This may seem a cold and calculating aspect to the day of romance you are planning, but it must be remembered that in the harsher times of our Celtic ancestors money and property was far harder to come by and seen as fixed, whereas love was understood by many to be transient, and just like today not all marriages lasted, for many various reasons. These were smaller closer-knit communities than the ones we live in today and any disputes over property or actions would be easier to prove. Not only would your witnesses of the day be local people, but others privy to your affairs would be likely to take sides should the relationship break down or be mutually terminated after the first year.

Some couples have the strangest clauses added to their contracts. I've seen one where the bride insisted that her husband agreed to always take out the rubbish every week and she in turn promised to iron his work shirts. Another had a clause that the bride would take complete control of all the finances and pay her husband a set amount of pocket money, he being a recovering gambler. Most of the property argued about in the past consisted of mutual homes and livestock, so if they managed to double their flock of sheep they could each claim fifty percent of the extra bred throughout their time together.

Contracts helped couples to know exactly where they stood financially and avoided many disputes that could evolve without them. The earliest Celtic contracts would have been memorised by the ovate and witnesses, because writing as we know it didn't exist then. Only the priesthood had any form of written language and that was Ogham, reserved for marking graves, leaving secret messages for each other, and directions or names. Not until the arrival of Latin do we see any evidence for the written word being used for such purposes. This began as the exclusive domain of only a few scholars who knew how to read it, so enormous trust was placed upon those who did.

You can design your own contract regarding money and property and add any clauses you so wish as long as you are both happy to sign it, then, as with any written and signed contract, **it can be considered legally binding**—unlike the hand-fasting itself, which remains outside modern-day laws. You would be advised to procure at least one witness but it's preferable to get two if possible.

The drawing up of a contract can apply to any form of marriage. It is not considered to be essential in Celtic marriage but will lend an air of authenticity to the event. So, you have your priest and priestess and have decided on the date and location of the event. Now for the ceremony itself.

The mistletoe is the most sacred plant of the Druid path and although it is not essential that it plays a part in today's rites of passage it is traditional. Oak trees are also especially sacred to Druids, but if you cannot get access to a grove of oaks then some oak leaves will suffice. The holly should also be represented if you choose to hold your hand-fasting during the winter. Other trees thought appropriate are crab apple, hawthorn and birch. The modern apple owes its origin to our native crab apple and has long been associated with love. To cut one width-ways reveals a five pointed star, and lovers would often share apples this way to strengthen their bond together. The hawthorn is a tree of love and fertility. Bringing a sprig of blossom into the bed chamber on the night of the hand-fasting will ensure a prosperous and fertile marriage. This is very powerful tree magic though, so if you are not intending to start a family in the next few months leave the hawthorn outside. The birch represents new beginnings and it's a nice idea to drain some sap beforehand to drink or make some birch sap wine in spring to drink at the ritual. This act of reverence will give the couple a clean and pure start to their relationship from which to build.

Most Druid orders wear white for performing rites of passage and therefore as the couple being wed you may prefer to wear an alternative colour. Green or yellow are good choices for both bride and groom as they are seasonally appropriate colours for Beltane and Lammas, the seasons most often chosen as the festivals to hold hand-fastings.

The priest and priestess will have four attendants to call the directions or quarters and bless the elements. The actual format of the ritual will largely depend on the tradition of the particular order you belong to or have ascribed to for the occasion but it is very similar to the Wiccan one laid out in the previous chapter. As modern Wicca has evolved mainly from the Celtic tradition this is not surprising.

Apart from only casting the one circle and calling on a particular Celtic goddess or god, the rest is pretty much the same.

The choice of deity is important and any decent priest or priestess will have gone into your path in detail before the event to discuss such details. She or he will want to know which deities you normally work with and may require you to prove your relationship with them in some way. This is important as, when calling on these ancient powers, one must be respectful. To call upon the blessing of a force neither of you is familiar with could be detrimental and taken as an affront by the deity concerned.

If the weather permits it is traditional to hold an open air celebration of the marriage afterwards. Some couples like to keep the day as authentic as possible and choose food and wine appropriate for the day, so if you need inspiration I have included a few recipes towards the end of the book.

The jewellery chosen for the occasion needs consideration also and any of a silver Celtic design would be in keeping. There are silversmiths who specialise in the making of bespoke jewellery for these rites and a couple of these are listed under sources on page 143.

The majority of couples choosing a Celtic marriage nowadays are usually already on a Druid or Green path and definitely do want the spiritual element to be there. If you doubt the spiritual element but feel strongly environmental then you may still be able to get a Celtic wedding, but I personally would design the day on a more humanist and non-religious basis. The most important consideration is the love and commitment between the couple, but many Druids may turn you down if you lack spirituality.

The jumping of fires, as mentioned earlier, could occur in Scotland and broomsticks in Wales with greater emphasis being put on music and dancing.

Again the priestess or priest may be giving of their time voluntarily and unlike the modern Christian clergy they don't have free accommodation, or a wage, so please don't forget to give back in return. This follows the traditional path and will be appreciated.

Viking Weddings

We can only presume that Viking weddings were similar to Celtic in so far as they were held in the open air, as were all important ceremonies of northern persuasion. The Norse seriously believed that any matter of importance, including all rites of passage and judgements, should be carried out this way so as to ensure that all was open and above suspicion in full view of the gods. An interesting example of this is Parliament Hill in London. Once an island, it was thought to be a spot used by the Vikings who held important meetings there.

To follow the procedure to the letter as found in the sagas, it is customary for the groom to approach the father of the bride before proposing. If he and his family consider it a good match, then an offer is made for the bride. The bride's family then consider the offer and, if happy for the wedding to take place, they see if they can match it in a dowry. The wedding itself is nothing more than a declaration of this agreement in front of at least two witnesses, then the couple are declared husband and wife, followed by feasting and copious drinking, which could go on for several days.

The morning after the ceremony it was traditional for the groom to give his wife a gift, the keys to his property, and equal access to his funds. It was up to the witnesses to remember the terms of the contract and one would presume the more complicated this was the more witnesses were required. This was then drawn up as a written contract, the precursor to a modern marriage certificate or pre-nuptial agreement.

Today's Norsemen and women can imitate this type of wedding symbolically and some do. There are in fact many similarities to modern marriages.

The feasting and merrymaking afterwards make for much fun anyway, and it's nice to try to emulate the food and drink side of things. Costume is optional but looks great and the more authentic you try to be the more atmosphere you are lending to the event. How religious an affair you wish to make it is up to you. There is no evidence of circle casting or priests and officials, although Viking/Christian converts may well have had one.

Calling upon an appropriate god or goddess is permissible but not essential, but asking them all for their blessing of the marriage is entirely likely to have occurred. To divorce yourself from the agreement at any stage you simply declare your intent in front of either the same witnesses as at the wedding or new ones if this is not possible. All goods now have to be split between the parties—nothing much changes really.

If you haven't already realised, there's not a single mention of hand-fasting, although the Vikings may well have adopted it from the Celts and used it as many of those on a Northern path do today.

Roman Weddings

These were usually fairly complicated affairs but if you wish to replicate them today it can be done and often is. A simplified version would be to refrain from the customary month-long search on suitability of the couple by both families and get on with it.

The costume for the groom is a basic tunic and leather sandals. The tunic can be made of expensive material if you want, but it doesn't really matter except to avoid man-made fabrics with the exception of silk. He would wear his best belt and probably have a large buckle depicting the latest Emperor or a specific deity. He would have a ritual bath beforehand and anoint himself with relevant oils.

The bride would have a special bridal gown prepared for this singular use and it was usually white. She wore a veil, most often red, and matching colour for her footwear. Her hair was divided into six locks and twisted to form a cone shape on the top of her head, supposedly to offer protection from evil forces. Her girdle consisted of three ropes and was tied in a complicated knot that was hard to undo. Hence the origins of today's expression of 'tying the knot'—perhaps it should be untying?

The custom of weddings in Rome was to hold them in the morning, with the entourage meeting first at the bride's house. Her father would hand her over to the groom, who paid his symbolic penny to his new father-in-law. They would then exchange words along the lines of *Ubi tu Gaius, ego Gaia*, or Where you are Gaius (male), I am Gaia (female). The matron of honour would then join their hands together and the couple would exchange rings, then raise their hands symbolically above before offering up a sacrifice, frequently a pig. To emulate this practice in Britain is illegal. Only registered abattoirs are permitted to do so.

The contract that had already been drawn up would now be presented to the bride by the priest and it was then signed by between five and ten witnesses depending on how high the status of the couple was. They all now sat down for a wedding breakfast, the food having been previously paid for by the groom, including the wedding cake, a simnel fruit cake that was broken over the couple's heads to ensure fruitfulness. Gifts were now presented to the couple by their guests.

After this they went through an elaborate gesture whereby the bride would be symbolically tugged from her mother's arms into the waiting arms of three of the groom's friends, the groom having already departed for his own property. The procession of the bride, her family and guests would now commence, bringing cheer to all en-route. Once arrived at her new home the bride would often make an offering of a domestic nature by the door to show her new status in society, and her groom would help her across in some form whilst they repeat the words exchanged earlier.

The couple would then go separately up to the bedchamber, bride first, and her mother who would help her undress and probably at this point give her some instant sex education such as, lie back and think of Rome dear.

Once the mother of the bride returns downstairs the groom would ascend and the couple would at last be alone. They were expected to consummate the marriage at this point but it wasn't obligatory. The feasting and merrymaking would continue downstairs below them. So it seems all you need for a Roman wedding is a priest, five witnesses, a contract, a penny, wedding attire, food and drink, and two homes within walking distance—and, of course, a consenting couple.

Humanist Weddings

Funnily enough the majority of people who approach me about hand-fastings are atheists looking for a non-religious ceremony. This in itself would normally be frowned upon by most of today's pagan community. I prefer not to be so biased: as long as the couple are devoted and serious in their intent, then why shouldn't they have the option to hand-fast? And who knows what the day could open up to them.

I would obviously remind them that they can obtain a legal marriage at their local registry office but it is often this that puts them off. Not everyone these days wants that as their only alternative and many turn to the pagan world for help. If their love for each other is the only spiritual element to be present deliberately then it seems a good enough starting point for me. It is important that both of them are equally keen to be hand-fasted, any reticence being considered as a reason for me to advise them to go home and think about it.

Considering that we know most ancient weddings were indeed very simple affairs and the religious aspect came later in our history as a pre-requisite for marriage, I feel it is perfectly ethical to carry out such a ceremony. The only content-related advice I can offer to anyone approached in such a way is to let the couple themselves design their day. As a rough guide, however, I would ask some simple questions regarding, location, guests and suitability on all counts. Non-religious hand-fastings can be as simple or complicated as the couple want and their imaginations and budgets allow. Questions you may wish to ask are:

1. Where?
2. When?
3. Officiated or not?
4. Guests?
5. Reception/party after?

A popular form of humanist wedding is to hold it at a venue of significance to the couple or just somewhere they really like, either indoors or outside, and to have a briefed officiate. The role of such a person is to introduce the couple to their guests and to state their intention to marry, as well as any hand-fasting required. The couple then take it in turns to declare their love and feelings for one another, after which they are declared married and bound.

Here is an example of a non-religious ceremony held on a beach in summer. The couple's names are Roddy and June they have been together for three years now and have a two year old daughter, Lucy, who is also present. They arrive with guests at mid-day (their choice), complete with barbecue and wine for afterwards. Roddy is dressed in his birthday suit as is June and most of their guests. Again this was their choice. As regular naturists they are used to such behaviour and the beach is a private one hired for the event. A friend (no, it wasn't me) officiates.

Friend: *Greetings everyone and thank you for being here today at Roddy and June's hand-fasting. June, you express a wish to become hand-fasted to Roddy today in front of your friends and family as a sign of your love and devotion to him. Is this so?*

June: *It is so.*

Friend: *Roddy you too have expressed a wish to become hand-fasted to June today in front of your family and friends as a sign of your love and devotion to June. Is this so?*

Roddy: *It is so.*

Friend: *June and Roddy, by binding your hands today we will be witnessing a strengthening of your commitment to each other and a deepening love. Are you happy with this?*

June: *I am.*

Roddy: *I am.*

Friend: *June, I would like you to read to Roddy the words you have written especially for him today.*

June: *Roddy, you are my enlightenment, you encourage me to shake off convention and embrace new experiences, you have widened my horizons and given me the most wonderful child. All this I thank you for, and love you deeply for, but most of all I thank you for loving me.*

Friend: *Roddy will you now please read the words you have chosen for June.*

Roddy: *June, I love you with all my heart and cannot imagine my life without you in it, you are my best friend, the mother of our child and my lover. I want you to think of this day as my declaration of total commitment to our love. May it last for ever.*

Friend: *June and Roddy, now you have said these words I will bind your hands together symbolic of the oneness you have found. I bind once, for you, June. I bind once, for you, Roddy. And lastly for your love together. Please feel free to kiss.*

They do this and are showered with rose petals brought along by family.

Friend: *June and Roddy, you are now hand-fasted and I ask you to be seated while we listen to a song sung by our minstrels here today.*

(They asked friends with musical ability to attend and play for them)

In this case the couple remained physically bound until all friends had been individually thanked for coming and the food was ready to be eaten, then they carefully placed the binding material (in this case ribbon) in a box prepared earlier. Now I don't for one minute want you to think that anyone having this sort of ceremony has to be skyclad (nude) and Roddy and June's wedding was a highly unusual but entertaining event by all accounts. Most humanist hand-fastings are of the fully-clothed variety but it made for an interesting example.

As a pagan I found this hand-fasting intriguing, for as much as the couple expressed their strong, almost evangelical, atheism they inadvertently emulated several spiritual practices not uncommon to us in today's pagan world.

They chose a beautiful outdoor location.

They chose to be skyclad or naked, considered a Gardnerian custom.

They expressed eloquently their love for each other.

They used rose petals as confetti.

They ate food prepared on an open fire.

All the elements were present, earth (sand), air (the wind), fire (the barbecue), and water (the sea).

Although the word 'spirit' didn't come into it, the day apparently felt very spiritual, to those aware of it, ironically.

Most couples then have some sort of post-wedding celebration and many have a honeymoon as in the traditional sense.

Like any hand-fasting this wedding is not a legal one and couples wishing to become legally married should be advised to go to their local civil office where they can also have a non-religious ceremony.

The Binding and Unbinding

The actual binding of a couple's hands causes some confusion, and again is disputed, but it is important to remember there are no proper or improper ways of doing it. The binding is symbolic and therefore can represent different things to different couples and their particular path or paths.

For couples going through a ceremony of betrothal, I would recommend a simple wrap rather than an actual binding, leaving the tying of the knot for your subsequent hand-fasting—if you end up having one that is. You can place as much importance on the method employed as you wish and may feel drawn to a particular style. For some people the emphasis of the ceremony is the literal physical joining, so more thought as to how you wish to be bound needs considering.

For those on a Wiccan or eclectic path, the choice of three wraps consecrated with an actual knot may be applicable, representing the forces you work with and your physical union as one. For my ceremonies I prefer this method as it is the most adaptable, but I am not averse to trying new ways and it was whilst working out a method to suit one couple that I came up with what I now call my Celtic knot. Most celebrants I have interviewed or spoken to invented their own methods, which may surprise you, but we have very little to go on histori-cally and all methods are correct.

Some bindings are very complicated, involving more than just the couple themselves, and can incorporate the elementals and other guests; but most opt for just the couple themselves. The simplest of formats and by far the most popular is for the priestess/priest or officiate to gently wrap and tie the chosen binding material either once or three times around the outside of the couple's clasped left hands at the mid-point where their thumbs join. This is done with the couple facing one another and holding their left or right hands as if they were about to shake them.

There is also some confusion regarding whether to place the binding on top of the couple's hands to begin with or the bottom. As it doesn't really matter to the gods or goddesses how you become bound, I wouldn't get too concerned, but it is easier in my limited experience to start by laying the binding midway over the top of the hands.

Tying the knot itself presents new questions: should it be one knot or two, should it be tied in a pretty bow, and does it really matter? Well it might, to you. I think tying it in line with the thumbs looks OK and allows people to still see your rings, but you may feel strongly about above or below. If we think of above being symbolic of expansiveness and below representing security, then decide which of these symbolisms is more impor-tant to you. Do you as a couple feel your relationship is one of mutual exploration and expansiveness or of connecting to the Earth? Maybe both? Tying somewhere midway is probably the safest option and covers most people's needs.

I personally think we can get too bogged down in these details and over-complicate what should be a relatively simple ceremony; but do what you will, safe in the knowledge that whatever you do will be what's right for you. If you still have doubts and your chosen priest or priestess doesn't have his or her own way of doing it, then try visualising that part of the ceremony during a planned meditation. This way you'll get the guidance *you* personally need.

Many Wiccan formats insist on three wraps, symbolic of the goddess, god and finally for their love, whether it be for a year or as long as it lasts. Some goddess-oriented ceremonies see this as symbolic of the three-phase Maid, Mother and Crone and will state this whilst binding. The binding can either be this simple three-fold twist or actually tied off.

To replicate my Celtic knot design takes some practice but looks aesthetically stunning; this can be achieved with five wraps representing the elements plus the spirit. To do this one starts by wrapping on the female side by the wrist going towards the little finger, then around to the male side repeating the same movement in reverse. As you come around again, go under the male and female thumbs, coming around again diagonally towards the female's fingers and around again to form a cross around his fingers, tying two simple reef knots at the bottom, and gently leaving any surplus material loose. I like to tie off at the bottom, as it looks better and I personally feel most couples need a symbolic grounding at this stage of the ceremony.

Some couples prefer to hold wrists and many northern traditionalists seem to prefer this type of position, again using the couple's left hands. The number of windings differs widely, so really it is up to you, but once is often enough for today's Norsemen and women. They also seem to opt for securing underneath.

For couples holding an eternal hand-fasting, the figure of eight symbolic of the loop of eternity is used. To achieve this, the binding material is made of one continuous thread or ribbon that is placed between the couple's hands in a cross. Once in position, their hands are joined and the remaining material is bound around their hands, either once, thrice or five times depending on their tradition, and secured above and below—symbolic of their eternal spiritual union.

A variation of the eternal binding is for the couple to face one another, holding both hands diagonally, creating their own physical figure of eight, allowing the priestess or priest to bind at the point of this cross in any way they so wish. Another method of handholding is for the couple to place their hands equally flat together and just allow each finger to slip in place next to the other with wrists pressed against the other. This will allow the priestess or priest to bind the wrists, but this isn't very comfortable for long periods.

These are a few of the many varied ways in which the actual binding can take place and I hope they offer some guidance and/or inspiration for you. As already mentioned the material is very much up to you, but silk ribbons are the most popular and keep indefinitely. When deciding the length of your binding material I would advise at least two to three feet for all but the eternal binding, which may have to be twice that length. Practice with string first to get it right.

Unbinding

For any couple wishing to unbind at some point in the future, it is quite simple. First, go back to the person/people who bound you and ask if they can perform an unbinding. They will obviously want to establish that the relationship is definitely over before going ahead and some, including myself, would recommend they wait at least a month before committing to the ritual. Any contracts and clauses thereof must be re-negotiated regarding joint possessions so the couple can separate with the minimum of discord. The most important issue will be the arrangements for any children resulting from the union and their future happiness and security.

Once these details have been discussed, if the couple are still intent on parting a suitable date will be set for the ritual unbinding.

For some traditions it will be important to include any previous witnesses if feasible, and the original binding material also if you still have it.

Each priestess or priest will have their own way of performing this important ceremony, which is usually far briefer and more solemn than the original fasting.

The importance of unbinding cannot be stressed strongly enough, as two souls once bound will continue together in sadness as well as happiness. If not, great melancholy or even illness in extreme cases can often result. I have a friend who became hand-fasted to his partner after they had been together for about a year. Two years later she decided the relationship wasn't working for her and broke it off, but without unbinding. My friend tried to get her to perform a separation ritual so they could both be released spiritually from each other but she refused. It transpired that she didn't take the hand-fasting seriously in the first place despite the full ritual they went through, and saw no need for any further 'hocus pocus', as she put it.

My friend had a dreadful time of it and found himself quite ill through the attachment they still had. It also made it difficult for him to attract new love. Eventually, though he wasn't happy with the situation, he performed a solitary unbinding to release his own spirit from its torment. Ironically his ex-partner also had a dreadful time of things and one wonders if she still is?

If you cannot arrange to use your original officiate, priestess or priest for whatever reason, and this may well be the case, then I advise you to perform your own ritual. This can be achieved fairly easily, depending on the kind of ceremony you had originally. If a circle was cast and energy raised, then try to duplicate this calling on the same energies or deities yourselves. Ask that they recognise your intent to go separately but peaceably into the world with no blame or judgement, and thank them for the love you once shared together. You can symbolically cut through the binding material and bury the pieces separately, along with any resulting bad feelings of the marriage. If yours was a non-spiritual ceremony, then get together on a pre-arranged day to state your unbinding and all the new arrangements that must now be put in place for your individual separate lives. This symbolic act can be of great use to couples who wish to remain friends, as well as making it easier to cope with the prospect of adjusting to a new form of relationship if children are involved.

We may not always like it, but once children are born to a couple they will invariably find their lives are still co-existent through the kids. Just because a couple aren't living together any more doesn't mean they won't still have to have some sort of parental relationship, and as it is usually the children who are the biggest victims of all relationship breakdowns it's vital that some amenable compromises can be found. Going through a ritual unbinding can heal many emotional wounds, which is why I would advise you to choose a strong waning moon and if possible hold the ceremony near some form of natural well or stream.

Occasionally couples will break down their barriers under such powerful spiritual energy and find themselves making up rather than breaking up. This is good.

4

Hand-fasting Accessories

Many of you on a pagan path may already possess a ritual robe, and it is perfectly alright for you to use this for your hand-fasting unless it is black. Black is not considered an auspicious colour to be wed in, but if you insist then use it.

Alternatively you can adapt clothing for the purpose or buy new either off the peg or hand made especially for the occasion. Most people seem to think that it is unlucky to wear an existing garment, but this is purely superstition, although from a spiritual standpoint I would advise against wearing any garment that previously belonged to a divorcee—for obvious reasons. I also feel that wearing clothing or objects connected to the deceased, unless they lived a happy life and died in natural circumstances, is inadvisable. If this seems confusing then let me explain. If granny leaves you her wedding dress and passed away peacefully but had an unhappy marriage would you wear it?

You may like to jazz up your attire a little for the occasion and many people like to either buy special jewellery or have it made. A special cloak pin or necklace could be acquired, but usually couples opt for rings. By adapting the traditional Gimmel ring of Tudor times a goddess ring can be made. Instead of the three parts being representative of the holy trinity, they can be of the three phases of the goddess or moon. Couples following a Celtic path often choose to use a *Claddagh* or Irish ring worn inverted as a sign you were available. If worn upright, married. These are easy to obtain from most high street jewellers.

There are no set designs for hand-fasting rings and you are free to express yourself any way you wish, but including some relevant markings even if the bands are plain will make them special to you and unique. Some couples like to opt for a design based on the elements, with some opting for chalices and others swords, pentagrams or wands. Suns and moons are also popular, as are runic markings for those of a northern persuasion.

Men are frequently drawn to the idea of wearing antlers for such occasions; this is possible but not that practical. Antlers are heavy and cumbersome and most definitely not designed for our heads, but if it works for you then fine, go ahead. An alternative would be to procure such headgear and leave it standing behind the groom during the ceremony as a relevant back drop.

Brides may wish to wear a garland of flowers in their hair and the easiest way of doing this is to use copper wire (not plastic coated garden wire) measured about four inches longer than the circumference of your head, which will allow you to twist the ends together.

Around this you can wind reeds or grass and incorporate blossom and flowers of your choice. I recommend you read up on the magical properties of trees and flowers, two examples of which can be found in further reading at the end of the book. The colours you choose for your wedding attire can be seasonally appropriate, e.g. green for Beltane or yellow for Lammas.

Ideally the cloth you choose should be man-made, not artificial, as should the binding material. Silk ribbons are acceptable, and decorated with silk leaves and flowers make for a lasting memento of the day. It is nice to prepare a small box in advance to contain this afterwards. It prevents you losing it, and by placing it in your box together you are again taking care to protect the binding. Keeping this under the marriage bed is thought to be auspicious.

Some Wiccans like the people responsible for calling the quarters to wear something of the colour pertaining to the element they are responsible for, and one couple I know had a local potter make up simple pendants of green, yellow, red and blue for this. If you are concerned with protection then placing suitable herbs such as rosemary and sage around your circle will help, as will the burning of suitable home-made incense on the altar.

The priest or priestess chosen for the day will discuss all these details with you in advance, and should encourage you to make as much as possible for yourself. It's *your* day, after all.

Some couples like to have a little gift for each of their guests ready at the end of the ceremony, and exchanges such as these are very popular and traditional. The gift doesn't have to cost much but if you have made it yourselves then it will strengthen the luck of the recipient. Home-made sweets wrapped in small pouches are nice and originate from a traditional Viennese custom in medieval times known as wedding favours.

Like all weddings, hand-fastings need pre-planning and preparation, so depending on how large an affair you want it to be you need to decide how far ahead to start. Obviously for most couples the decision to 'do it' is the first step but there are many other considerations including invitations.

An invitation to a hand-fasting can be shop-bought or hand-made. I know of one couple who even went to the lengths of making their own paper for this! If the budget allows, you could have some specially printed up. It could look something like the following.

Megan Griffiths & Neil Jones

Invite you to their Hand-Fasting

To be held on Tuesday 1 May

At Longbarrow Meadow
Newlodge
Greenshire

from 11.30 am to sunset

RSVP

Ideally the longer notice you give people the better, a year being thought long enough but six months is probably the shortest time you should allow.

Something we haven't touched on up until now is the compatibility of family and spiritual friends. Many modern pagans have non-pagan family and friends to consider, so it's important you inform them fully of what to expect in case any of them object to being a part of it. This is especially relevant when attending a magical ceremony during which circles are cast and energy is raised. The last thing any couple need is uncle John collapsing in hysterics and reducing your day to ridicule.

Most couples I know are sensitive to this likelihood and to avoid problems will either have a civil wedding that all can attend, including the uncle Johns of this world, and a separate day of spiritual hand-fasting for their pagan family or coven. If you are lucky enough to be surrounded only by spiritual people then this doesn't have to be a consideration.

For any couple who prefer not to legally marry but do want a spiritual hand-fasting, then my only advice is to think very carefully about whom you invite and make sure everyone attending is made fully aware of what it will entail. One way around this predicament is to ask the priest or priestess to print out the ceremony in advance and send a copy of it to all your expected guests—forewarned is forearmed—and you can then stress the seriousness of the ritual and any potential protagonists will hopefully be put off coming.

The altar is an important part of the day and you need to think ahead regarding what you will be using as one. You might be lucky enough to be using somewhere that already has a natural altar available, such as a bench or stone slab, but for most people it involves having to take one with them, the size and weight of which will largely depend on how far you have to walk once you arrive at your destination. I know of one couple that fell madly in love with a secret meadow tucked away on the far side of some ancient coppiced woodland, but sadly had to relinquish their desire to hold their hand-fasting in this beautiful spot because it would have been entirely impractical to do so. Not only would it have meant dragging all the 'bits' they needed with them, but for the more elderly and unsteady members of their coven it would be an impossible trek. Reluctantly they settled for the entrance of the woods and the natural cover of an already existing work area and fire, but in the end it made for a sensible alternative, offering direct access to the car park and facilities. So that they could still use the meadow in some capacity they gained permission to sleep there for the wedding night and literally honey-mooned under the full moon.

The altar can be as simple as a pasting table covered with an appropriate cloth or in the above case we used two oak stools with an ash bench placed on top which sufficed very well for the occasion. You will need to negotiate with your intended priest or priestess over the items you place on it and make sure they are put in the relevant positions, i.e. earth in the north, air in the east, fire in the south and water in the west. Your priest or priestess might prefer to use his or her own ritual tools for the ritual and may object to using yours, so don't be surprised or offended.

The very basics you will require are a wand, athame, broom or sword to cast the circle (this should really be the priest's or priestess's domain), a container with earth or sand in it or crystals, rose quartz being a good choice and easily obtainable from most high streets these days. You will need at least one candle and it's a good idea to bring a glass jar or similar to put this in to prevent it being blown out. For the air element, either use some incense (home-made being preferable) or feathers, and finally a chalice or suitable receptacle for holding water. Ideally the water should be pure well water but rain water or tap water can be used and sprinkled with sea salt to purify it.

One very important item not to be excluded is an offering, especially relevant if gods and goddesses are being called. Finding an appropriate item needs careful consideration as it should not only relate to love but to the god and goddess concerned. You may already have something in mind, but if not too sure then consult your priest or priestess who should be happy to guide you in the right direction. The sacrifice of something special thrown into a well, pond, river or the sea if feasible, is very traditional and stems from the bronze age. This magical act was especially relevant from an elemental standpoint, water being the element associated with love. It is still believed to bring luck and operates on a sliding scale of intensity based on the value of the object being sacrificed. The higher its value to you the greater the magical effect and the bigger the reward theoretically.

Interestingly the word sacrifice comes from the Latin *sacrificare*, to give up, as in 'to the gods'. At its most basic and simplest, the offering could take the form of a clay goddess model and phallic symbol for the god. Food is often thought a good form of offering, as are flowers (but not a tin of beans and cut flowers from the market!). The spirits prefer all things natural and the more effort you put into making or growing your own the better, so a bunch of home-grown roses and some home-made heart-shaped biscuits or cookies would be better.

If you follow a particular tradition they will have their own customs to adhere to, but be careful not to inadvertently mix your path's, for example don't hold a Celtic hand-fasting and wear Nordic jewellery. This will be seen as an insult to the powers that be! Having another table covered and simply dressed with foliage found in the location on the day, for guests to leave their offerings or presents on, is a good idea but always remember to ask first before helping yourself and thank afterwards. This refers to both the owner (if there is one) of the land you are on as well as the actual spirit of whatever tree or shrub you are about to sever bits from.

Seating for guests outside is a very important issue and expecting your guests to stand or just sit on damp earth is not a good idea. Some might not mind but for others it could prove problematic, so sorting out these details in advance will pay off. You might have to bring some form of seating with you or arrange for a friend to prepare this before you arrive. At the very least bring blankets or picnic sheeting just in case, to avoid embarrassment.

I don't mean to sound patronising, but the lighting of fires is very tempting but doesn't always go down well, so if planning to light one check first that it will be OK. Fires can get out of control, so have a bucket of water or sand handy just in case. This is extremely relevant if holding your hand-fasting during an especially dry period. You don't want to be responsible for starting a localised catastrophe and find your hand-fasting making headline news for all the wrong reasons.

Having a simple first aid kit will also be useful, as people can have minor accidents, especially if consuming large quantities of alcohol.

The weather can be unpredictable to say the least in this country, so prepare for the worst and if possible have some form of cover available should rain or worse occur.

Lastly I have prepared a simple check list for you to use as a rough guide that covers the basics, but most of all I wish to emphasise that this is your day and as such should be *your* day. Use it well and it will remain a beautiful experience you will both remember for the rest of your lives.

1. Priest, priestess or officiate
2. Location location location
3. Date, time and invitations
4. Type, path/spiritual or otherwise.
5. Contract or not
6. Certificate or not
7. Equipment and/or ritual tools
8. Clothing and jewellery
9. Offerings and/or gifts
10. Food and drink
11. Flowers
12. Cake
13. Budget

Personal planning pages can be found on pages 121 onwards.

Ritual Guidance

If the reason you are reading this book is because you have been asked to perform a hand-fasting and need guidance, then relax while we take a more intensive look into the ritual. It is not necessary for you to be a fully initiated priestess or priest. The bulk of today's pagans are uninitiated so you are in good company.

First let's look at exactly what constitutes an initiated person these days. An initiated person is someone who has reached the point on their spiritual journey where they feel the need to dedicate and pledge allegiance to a particular path or coven and declare themselves magical people. This is achieved by the performance of an initiating ceremony or ritual. The potential initiate will be invited by either their coven or mentor to undergo such a ritual when the time is right for them, usually after one to three years of study and practice of their chosen craft. For the solitary practitioners, who by and large make up the majority of pagans today, the decision to self-initiate is the only alternative.

I came to this point about four years ago after approximately one conscious year of deliberate practice, although I had been spiritually aware for at least two years preceding and had been inadvertently following my path subconsciously all my life. The decision to tread a green path was made for me by the spirit of the Green Man who had always been close to me since childhood, not surprising for someone brought up on the edge of such an inspiring place as ancient Epping Forest.

The choice of path or tradition, unless hereditary (not an easy one to prove), is usually obvious to the individual based on their own beliefs, feelings and what they are drawn to. Some instinctively 'feel' Celtic, choosing to 'work' with a particular god or goddess, some Norse and for many these days Wicca. But you do not have to tread these specific paths at all and therefore a large proportion of today's practising pagans are eclectic.

For those of you unfamiliar with terms such as 'practising' and 'working' let me explain. Practising means that you actively pursue a spiritual life by means of example in awareness of spirit, showing reverence to nature, love and greater under-standing of self and others, and generally aspire to be essentially as harmless as is possible. It also refers to the optional learning of particular magical arts such as meditation or path workings, healing, raising spiritual energies, celebration and understanding of festivals and moon phases, divination, result magic (spells), rites of passage, creativity, and most importantly self belief amongst many others.

Working is when we refer to a specific magical act, often carried out ritualistically. Whether it is as simple as giving unbiased objective advice to someone during a reading, planting a tree and blessing it or carrying out a high magical rite in a coven, it is all considered work. Working with invoked (called upon) magical energies such as specific ancient deities happens for a variety of reasons. Sometimes these ancient forces will approach you first either during meditations or you can stumble upon them out walking, for example, or you may actively seek them out. Whichever way it happens, you must try to be calm, taking note of any message you feel they may have for you. Even if this doesn't occur you may still be drawn to a particular force because of an affinity you feel for it or a quality you need from it.

The one thing to remember when 'working' with any energetic being, from the dizzy heights of Thor to the humble spirit of your home, is that you must treat them with respect. By actively connecting with the spirit world we open ourselves up on a different and magical level and therefore any traditional practices should be adhered to. The Celtic and northern paths have a rule of a gift for a gift, meaning if you ask them to do something on your behalf then they will expect you to give in return. This doesn't necessarily mean directly to them, but if for example you ask for money and it works then they might expect you to give some to a charity or other cause you deem virtuous.

So how can you perform the magical rite of hand-fasting if you are not initiated? The answer to this is simple. You can if you are already familiar with (i) raising spiritual energy through medita-tion, (ii) invoking deities and (iii) protection or circle casting. If not, then it will require you to become so before attempting to perform the rite. The only exception to this is if the couple want a spiritual flavour but are not worried about raising energy.

There are numerous books you can read for basic guidance and courses to go on, so if in doubt of your knowledge or ability contact the Pagan Federation who should be happy to help. Their address is under sources on page 143.

To prepare yourself for the event, meditate on all the elements first and see what they reveal to you, keeping a record of these insights as you progress. Call on the forces you normally work with and write down their responses.

Practise casting big circles if you are not used to it, and if possible familiarise yourself with the intended venue by opening up to the energy of the space and getting a feel of it.

Make sure you have something suitable to wear. It is not necessary to use a cloak and robe but they do look right and are generally what is expected. Women can have an easier time of it where this dilemma is concerned, by choosing to wear a long dress, suitable for the occasion, instead. Use your normal tools and prepare them in advance by cleansing them beforehand. Spend time with your couple and, if you don't already know, then find out as much as you can about their beliefs. Familiarise yourself with the forces they wish you to work with or suggest they use an energy you already work with. Chances are that's why they chose you originally.

The basis for any ritual is to open, enter and close, so you need three energy points: (i) the initial opening ceremony allowing access to the veiled world of magic, (ii) the ceremony of love itself when vows are exchanged and hands fasted and (iii) the closing and exiting of the magical world by thanks and farewells.

The protective circle contains any energy raised and the energy within it whilst preventing any negative forces from entering. By calling upon the four elementals we are practising elemental magic, which allows those forces to be present and both strengthens the couple with their qualities and allows for the basic energetic components to be in place for any ritual, blessings, cleansings, enhancing and inspirations to happen, as called for or required through the words chosen to call upon them. I personally find that earth offers structure, air conveys the original thought, fire gives the energy and passion and water allows movement of love in hand-fastings.

Invoking a specific deity allows the force of that manifest being to be present again to energise, bless, cleanse, and so on. Invoking the goddess and god of Wiccan faith has much the same effect but will feel different to each individual present. The whole point of a magical ritual like this is to spiritually strengthen, bind and unite the couple, adding its own unique extra dimension to the occasion.

Broken down very simply it is as follows.

1. The circle is cast of protective light energy raised by the priestess, often carried out physically with a broom, sword, wand or athame in a doesil (clockwise) direction from north if a north-oriented altar or east if an eastern-oriented one, the two being favourite in the northern hemisphere. The circle is symbolically 'put out there' three times and it is normally important to contain the circle by the holding of hands or understanding of those in it that it must not be broken during the ritual. It is not essential to cast a circle, but creating a spiritual protective (usually blue or purple) light of love in your mind's eye around the congregation will suffice, and if you prefer this method no-one but yourself will be aware of your magical actions.

2. The couple are introduced, plus any planned reading. Some people like a dramatic entrance including the opening of a magical door in the circle, the crossing of a broom, or opening of an actual physical door. Others opt for simply placing everyone in their places in advance. I prefer a middle road, placing my couple within the sacred space at south and asking them to walk towards me, thus:

Bride's name *and* **Groom's name**, *I invite you to step forward and join us today in performing this your sacred rite of hand-fasting.*

3. The elementals are called upon literally or symbolically by use of four 'quarters' or helpers, already placed in their correct positions. The elements should be represented in some way. I like to hold each elemental in turn whilst calling upon it so I have a very nice consecrated quartz obelisk that I use for earth, a swinging censer (yes, like a church one) filled with whatever incense the couple have chosen to use, a candle, normally white, and the chalice of blessed pure spring water. To call upon elementals is quite easy if you have spent time and practised meditating on them before. Simply tune in to the energy of that element by focusing on it physically and then go with it and it will reveal itself in whatever way is appropriate for you.

The calling can be done so:

I call upon the Spirits of the North of the Earth oh blessed ancient rock that we live upon that has seen all and knows all and contains our secret origins like precious jewels be here and make solid today the joining in love of **Bride's name** *and* **Groom's name.**

All: *With grateful thanks I feel your presence.*

I call upon the Spirits of the East of the Air oh blessed breath that we take in that inspires us and creates form and contains our secret origins like whispers of truth be here and focus our thoughts today in the joining in love of **Bride's name** *and* **Groom's name.**

All: *With grateful thanks I feel your presence.*

I call upon the Spirits of the South of Fire oh blessed Sun that shines down on us and rises our passions and contains our secret origins rising like a phoenix from the flame be here and warm our hearts and souls today in the joining in love of **Bride's name** *and* **Groom's name.**

All: *With grateful thanks I feel your presence.*

I call upon the Spirits of the West of the Water oh blessed Moon that moves our tides and governs our emotions and contains our secret origins like its shadow cast across the land be here and let love flow freely today in the joining in love of **Bride's name** *and* **Groom's name.**

All: *With grateful thanks I feel your presence.*

The couple will either be asked to visit each 'human' quarter in turn for a blessing or come up to the altar to be blessed, and cleansed if required, by the priestess or priest by the represented elements.

4. The priestess or priest asks each of the couple their intent and establishes their mutual consent. This can be put as:

Do you, **Bride's name***, wish today to start a life of love, respect and trust with* **Groom's name***, and are you ready to do this knowing all that it will possibly entail?*
(ditto for groom)
I call the witness of the bride.
(ditto for groom)

They normally stand either side of the couple and if there are any pre-nuptial contracts to sign the respective witnesses can read each part if required. I would advise against this if the contract is an especially long one. The contract is signed by both witnesses and the couple.

You can then ask them to be seated again.

5. The invocation by the priestess or priest of specific goddess or god or both. There are various ways in which one can invoke. I personally like to spend time tuning myself into the energy in advance by process of meditation. Some people like to symboli-cally 'draw' invocation pentagrams in the air facing the direction relating to the deity they are invoking whilst calling their name, but this is not necessary. Some face the altar and others face the congregation using a goddess stance, legs apart and arms spread uplifted apart, or god stance, legs closed and arms crossed over chest looking upward, depending on the deity or dieties they are invoking. Goddess energy usually comes up from below through the base chakra and god energy from above or crown

chakra in my experience. Some like to hold their athame, sword or wand some not—its up to you, but if you have an invocation that you use regularly then use it, adapting where needed. I feel that as long as you are 'open' to the energy the 'calling' itself is usually all that is required. The words themselves have power, as does the name of the deity you are calling. If the conditions are right they will 'appear'—not necessarily in the physical sense, although this is possible, but in some way the energy of the space will feel different, even to the uninitiated, as if something far more loving and powerful than us is present. We all have our own methods and whether you have learnt them from a mentor, coven or through your own solitary practice they are all equally valid. So hopefully by the time you are ready to do this you should already be flowing with divine energy and only have to call upon them by name, believing one hundred percent that they will respond. The response is sometimes obviously manifested or can be subtler, depending on what they feel is required, and it can be done thus:

OH **deity or deities** *of* (whatever descriptive prose is appropriate) *to be here today in this sacred space to join us in celebrating the joining in mind, body and spirit of* **Bride's name** *and* **Groom's name**, *bathe us in your divine power and honour us with your presence and energy throughout this ritual until the time comes that we must say farewell. So mote it be* (optional).

6. The couple are invited to make their vows plus any further readings or songs. Normally the couple will be standing in front of you at this point with their backs to your group, so ask them to face one another. You can say something like:

Bride's name, *I invite you to face* **Groom's name** *with love and honesty to make the vows of intent for your relationship in full view of your family, friends, the elemental spirits and* **goddess or god**, *who are here today to offer their light, love and blessings to this spiritual union.*
(Repeat for groom) Vows are made, bride first.

7. Rings and personal spiritual gifts, if any, are exchanged and the priestess or priest performs the actual hand-fasting. Some people like the idea of having a best/first man and best/first lady to bring the rings to the couple on a cushion but it's up to you. If you decide against this then one can simply ask for the priestess or priest to have them ready on the altar or otherwise. Normally the priestess or priest will say a few words along these lines:

Bride's name, *Please take the ring you have for* **Groom's name,** *and place it on his chosen finger* (this can be any one you like but most people opt for the traditional) *saying these words.*

Bride: *I give you this magical ring to wear as a symbol of the love between us and the spiritual bond we have as one.* (Repeat same process for groom)

After this ask the couple if they have any special gifts for each other and invite them to exchange them, each saying a few words explaining what the gift is for and why they are giving it. Now it remains for you to bind their hands in the manner you have already practised and agreed to. It is important to announce this bit a little louder to emphasise the importance of this spiritual heart of the ceremony such as:

Bride's name, *You have expressed your intent, made your vows, exchanged your rings and offered gifts in the name of the love you share with* **Groom's name,** *and in the love and light of everyone here in the presence of* **invoked deity** (plus any reverent description of said being: for example, the great mother goddess etc.)
and
Groom's name, *You have expressed your intent, made your vows, exchanged your rings and offered gifts in the name of the love you share with* **Bride's name,** *and in the love and light of everyone here in the presence of* **invoked deity** (plus any relevant description again). *By the power of your love for each other, those that you love and love you, in the name of* **invoked deity,** *I ask you to join your left* (or right, or both) *hands as I bind you with this cord today once for*

(fill in as required), *twice for* (if applicable) *and thrice etc. For a year and a day* (betrothals), *for* (set period), *for as long as love survives or for ever (*state which as applicable).

You are now hand-fasted and are bound as one together in love, light and understanding. Let no one come between you and may your union be one of love, respect and consideration to each other and all living things from this day forth.

8. The couple are encouraged to embrace and/or kiss. Blessings from invoked energy or energies and priestess or priest are made. It would be almost impossible for me to guide you verbally on this subject, as I cannot possibly know which energy or energies you are planning on calling, but you can introduce it by saying something like:

I bless this couple in the name of **invoked deity**, *wishing you a happy, healthy loving future on your path together as one.*

Priestess or priest may choose to touch the point of the binding at this point with an athame, wand or sword but could choose just to use his or her hands. Any spiritual personal gift could be given at this juncture also.

10. Reading from priestess or priest (which can be anything from a poem to a more personal message from the priestess or priest and is very much down to personal preference).

11. The giving of thanks and farewells to invoked energy or energies. This is very easy but must be done and can be put thus:

We give light, love and gratitude to **invoked deity** (plus descriptive prose as before) *for blessing us with your divine energy and blessing the hand-fasting of* **Bride's name** *and* **Groom's name** *here today and now must bid you farewell.*

12. The giving of thanks and farewells to the elements or quarters. If you have human quarters then face each one in turn from north or east depending on the orientation of your altar. If not then face the altar and bid farewell that way instead. For human quarters you can say:

With light, love and thanks for your presence here today and we bid farewell to you the Spirit of the North of Earth

then nod respectively as they nod back in acknowledgement. (Ditto for the rest.) You can say pretty much the same when facing the altar but touch each one in turn as you do. Some couples are instructed to visit each quarter in turn whilst still bound as this is done, but it's optional.

13. Priestess or priest officially closes the ceremony, saying, for example:

All that is left is love and that is what we shall all take with us today as we leave this sacred space to celebrate further the joining of this magical couple in a life of spiritual harmony and unity. Blessings be to you all and farewell!

The couple may wish to be released from their physical binding at this point. Don't forget to close your own energy points afterwards. As with most views on circle casting it is not usually necessary to un-cast, as the protective light will fade on its own.

This is a basic formula that works and is usually quite easy to reproduce, the most important thing being to remember to relax and enjoy it. Be strong and positive, and practise projecting your most loving, caring, voice in advance so everyone will hear you on the day. I know someone who went to the lengths of putting cotton wool in her ears several hours before her first public ritual. Her temporary hearing deprivation ensured her voice sounded loud enough to all but her, ironically.

It is important to be prepared to open up completely to the energies you wish to raise and to some extent the role of priest or priestess is that of complete belief and trust in his or her abilities to do this. To expect to gain overnight success in this is unrealistic, as normally it takes years of practice, although for those totally walking the walk, as it were, and living a purely spiritual life, doors can open fairly quickly. Meditation is the key to learning how to raise spiritual energy and one needs to be reasonably proficient at it to succeed.

Your appearance on the day is important, and like the couple you are about to hand-fast you need to present yourself in a clean and pleasant manner. But contrary to the opinions of some it is not necessary to don the biggest pentagram you can find. If planning to enlist the use of others during the ritual, then have opportunities for everyone to meet beforehand and rehearse all their parts thoroughly. It is ultimately your responsibility to ensure everyone knows their roles and it is you they will look to if unsure. To avoid any lapses of memory print out the order of service in advance, letting all participants have a copy.

As priestess or priest it is up to you to give confidence and structure to the event, so keep yourself focused in the now during the ceremony and try not to get distracted. Make sure you are happy with the format and the words you intend using, trying if possible to commit them to memory. If unfamiliar with the ceremony you may have to approach it like an actor does. Method acting of course. There is a certain dramatic quality to these ceremonies so if you are not happy to be centre stage in rituals then back out gracefully and try to help your couple find someone else.

I am not going to go into depth on guiding you verbally as I personally feel only those concerned can really decide on how they wish to express their love. I will say, however, that you have the blessings and permission of the creators of the example rituals in this book to use any for guidance. It is perfectly permissible to draw from other people's ceremonies but bear in mind that your own words often carry the most power and hopefully most of them will be divinely inspired anyway.

Your couple may choose to give you a free rein on format and wording, trusting in your wisdom, but encourage them to create their own vows. These are words they will be promising spiritually to live by, so extra guidance and higher wisdom is required when making them, and the potential consequences of breaking them need considering also. Whatever you do don't say anything you are not happy with or go along with any ceremony that raises energy but doesn't close properly. If there are any serious doubts in your mind then think again before agreeing to doing it. There maybe someone else better placed than you to meet their requirements. It is also equally possible that, come the day, you will do such a brilliant job that you could find yourself being asked again and potentially it could snowball, so give these possibilities careful consideration.

To enter into the world of holding rites of passage may encroach on your everyday life more than planned and it could prove problematic. As far as charging is concerned I would let your conscience be your guide. If you instinctively feel it is wrong then don't do it and give selflessly. The universe is sure to give back in some way, but if on the other hand you see it as part of the way or the only way you earn a living then charge accordingly. The only advice I can give is to charge by what you feel you are worth on a sliding scale. If you feel you have something unique or special to offer then increase your worth slightly. This could be access to a recognised ancient sacred site or a high degree initiation from a well-known coven or path. If you are the only uniqueness to offer, then charge a mean average of all your hourly rates. If needing more insight then simply contact some of the popular priestesses or priests of your area through moots or the Pagan Federation and find out what they charge.

I also think it is a nice touch to bring a gift for the couple that you have blessed in advance. If you are exceedingly emotionally driven be prepared to keep a dry eye until after the event. Breaking down in tears of happiness is the domain of the respective parents, not ours, and looks very unprofessional. If properly charged with magical energy this shouldn't occur. For those of you unable as yet to feel confident in your ability to raise energy then don't offer what you can't deliver. It's better to save face and let them find someone more experienced. If your couple aren't particularly worried about this then go ahead, but your initial interview should tell both parties all they need to know about mutual suitability.

For anyone intending to officiate without deliberately raising energy (I say deliberately as many people do it uncontrollably!)

then you can follow the same basic structure in a simplified version, thus:

1. Open your ceremony by thanking everyone for attending. Explain briefly the origins of the ceremony; for example:

    We are here today to celebrate the love of .... and .... by performing the ancient Celtic tradition of hand-fasting in the joining of our couple as one in mind, body and spirit.

2. Ask the couple if they know any reasons why they should not be joined and then bless them alternately with the four elements describing why you do this as you do it, thus:

    I bless you .... with the element of Earth. May your physical needs be met and good health and fortune come your way.
    I bless you .... with the element of Air. May your love be inspired and your thoughts and words be truly honest and positive.
    I bless you .... with the element of Fire. May your love be passionate warm and as generous as the Sun.
    I bless you .... with the element of Water. May your emotional bonds grow with each cycle of the Moon.

3. Giving and receiving of rings and exchanging of pre-written vows with couple facing each other.
4. Any special readings and/or songs.
5. Perform the binding explaining as you go thus:

    .... and ...., you have asked me here today to perform the task of hand-fasting and now that you have declared your love for each other and made your sacred vows I ask you to join your left hands as I fast you once for ...., once for ...., and once for your souls now joined as one. As one you are stronger and can enjoy the dance of the male and female inside you.

6. Song or hymn of celebration if possible or reading by invited speaker if not.

7. Blessing by you thus:

   I bless you both on your path together, ready to face the world as a couple bound in love, freely, wildly, enthusiastically, thoughtfully, compassionately, honestly and if it is your wish may the union prove fertile (or along those lines).

8. Making of offerings placed either on the altar or in specially pre-decided spot, e.g. a well (make sure its eco friendly and permissible), and/or exchange of gifts.

9. Invite the couple to kiss.

10. Any broomstick jumping or fire jumping if planned. Some couples do a circuit of the perimeter of the space whilst still bound.

11. Thank everyone again for being there, declare the couple are hand-fasted then remove the binding if they wish you to, and announce the end of the ceremony.

12. Party!

It must be stressed that this is simply a guideline for you and you should really let your imaginations run free as far as your budgets will allow. The one thing I didn't want to do is lead you by the hand every step as my path is definitely mine and will invariably be different from yours, so use the first ceremony as guidance, if you need it, for wording on the second ceremony where appropriate. By seeking advice from someone more experienced you can get invaluable insights and ideas that books such as these cannot offer. There is nothing so good as first-hand experience. It is very flattering to be invited to hold a hand-fasting and reflects well on you that people in your sphere of influence see you as such a caring and responsible being. Enjoy it!

Final Preparations for the Couple

Most of you already familiar with ritual will instinctively prepare yourselves spiritually for the event by process of meditation and physical cleansing. You may also wish to purge or cleanse internally as well by de-toxing a few days before. For those of you unfamiliar with such practices I urge you to at least consider deeply the rite you are about to go through if you haven't already.

Whether you are spiritually aware or not, you will be declaring your intimate love and bonding to another in front of the universe as well as any family and friends present. Regardless of your path or beliefs you will still have your own conscience to deal with if indeed the marriage does fail, and this does need careful consideration.

This example serves to inform you of the depth of soul binding you will be going through by engaging in a spiritual hand-fasting. It is not necessary to be separate the night before, but I think it is a good tradition as it gives both parties a last chance to be alone with their thoughts and the true feelings of their hearts.

For those of you who opted for the traditional hen or stag night the night before, hangovers could be a problem and many a wedding starts this way, sadly. Spiritually this will leave you toxic and tired, not the best start to a life of wedded bliss! I would recommend such activities occur several nights before the planned day, allowing tradition to have its way but ensuring you make the event refreshed and ready.

A pre-wedding bath specially prepared with appropriate herbs, oils and flowers will relax you and set the mood, cleansing more than just your body. Don't use any perfumes or oils you are not familiar with, though, as the last thing you need is an allergic reaction to deal with and the prospect of greeting your loved one looking like a bloated lobster.

Make sure all your wedding attire is laid out ready the night before and any last-minute floral headgear can be put together just prior to setting off, providing the flowers are readily available, which they should be!

For those of you concerned with hair who are planning a special and elaborate style for the occasion, then getting a hair-dresser to visit at home is easiest and infinitely preferable to running around the district like a headless chicken getting panicky and flustered. It cannot be emphasised strongly enough that the more planning and preparation you put into the day, no matter how simple an affair you are having, the smoother it will go and the more you will be able to enjoy it.

As bride and groom you should try to delegate as many jobs as possible among family and friends, who hopefully will be only too pleased to help.

In an ideal world all you should have to worry about is turning up dressed and ready to be hand-fasted, with everything else just slipping into place. I would recommend you draw up a pre-wedding plan well in advance and update it as required as you get closer to the date. This plan should get smaller as you gradually account for all eventualities. To help you with this I have included pages for notes on the various requisites on pages 121 onwards.

Asking your priest or priestess for a pre-wedding blessing is a good idea and will help to strengthen your belief in the day and resulting union, so aiding positive energy to work in your favour.

I would definitely hand over the responsibility of last-minute food preparation to someone willing to do it, as cooking in bridal clothes is not to be recommended even if you have helped up till the day itself.

Recording Your Day

You may have drawn up a contract and or certificate to remember the day with and may also be planning to preserve your binding material in some way, but what about photography? Obviously our ancestors lacked this magical art but we have it and photographs of the day will, like any wedding pictures, be lasting mementos of your special day. You can of course hire a photographer for the occasion, but remember what was said earlier about mixing the non-pagan with pagan elements. If you are lucky enough to have a pagan or pagan-friendly photographer to use, then brilliant, but if not what are your options?

I would try to find someone among your family and friends to take the photos and use a decent camera if possible. Most SLR cameras have an automatic setting that makes them easy for anyone to use and they generally produce the best pictures. Any camera with a panoramic setting will be useful for larger group photos. Another very popular innovation is the digital camera, giving you instant access to your pictures directly after the event. Camcorders are widely used at all forms of weddings and again can give you immediate results, although they vary in quality widely, as do their users!

Your priest or priestess may possibly object to the rite itself being recorded as it could upset the elementals, so ask if you can pose in a circle briefly after the event as an alternative.

By the time you get to taking official photographs people will be getting hungry, so keep it brief and efficient. I would recommend a large group photo, followed by bride and family, then groom and family, ending with bride and groom as the basic requirements. A close-up of the bride and groom's bound hands is a nice touch and one couple I know of thought this was the best photo of their hand-fasting. Adding this image to the bottom of your certificate, if you have one, is also a wonderful idea and can look stunning.

Of Minstrels and Music

Traditionally any feast held by our ancestors, no matter how poor or humble, had music. Whether it was the beat of the Irish *bodhran* (pronounced *boran*), or a simple tune played on the penny whistle, it all adds to the occasion. For modern-day pagans the options are more extensive and many couples choose a complete musical accompaniment.

In choosing your tunes be thoughtful of the path or tradition you are on and any traditional music associated with it. There are a great number of Celtic music recordings and musicians to choose from, for example, so if you don't already know what you want then check out your local music shop and ask to listen to a few in advance.

Ceilidh (pronounced *cailee*) bands are very popular for all sorts of occasions and for those of you having a Celtic theme these are entirely appropriate and great fun for your guests. They are similar to square dancing and everyone physically capable is encouraged to get up and join in.

You can of course use any music you like. Whether it's a pre-recorded tape put together specially for the event or a live band, it doesn't matter, but live music is better and more in keeping.

Most bands or musicians will expect to be paid for their hard work and it's important to allow for this in your budget. They will definitely appreciate lubrication, so keep them stocked up with drinks throughout the day and delegate this responsibility to someone. I personally feel the ritual itself should be fairly quiet, and maybe an opening tune and closing one is all that will be necessary. But if you want to go the whole hog and have it fully orchestrated then go ahead. Even if all you can afford is an acoustic folk singer it will still add another element of magic to the day. Traditional folk music is not everyone's cup of tea so bear in mind that you can choose any type of music you want providing it is happy and positive and preferably of love.

5

Hand-Fasting Hand-Feasting

Our ancestors especially welcomed feasting days and most would have observed the seasonal feasts as well as any additional rites of passage, with burial feasts being the most important. These days were an opportunity for the tribe or village to share the best of their produce and entertain visitors from other tribes and villages. By Anglo-Saxon times a day of fasting would precede the feast day as a mark of respect for both the newly adopted Christian God and, for those of more traditional persuasion, the old gods and goddesses of their ancestors.

As I have mentioned frequently, hand-fasting rituals would most likely be incorporated into the seasonal feasts of Beltane or Easter and Lammas or harvest time. Although I can find no accurate records of specific hand-fasting feasts, there are sources we can draw from to discover exactly what was eaten. The Anglo-Saxon period, particularly, has records of feasts and the food available, but to look farther back we have to rely on our imaginations, backed up with what little archaeological evidence remains.

Regional and seasonal variations occur throughout Britain, as with the rest of the pagan world. Pork was unlikely to have been consumed during summer months due to its tendency to go off rather quickly. Meat was a luxury and beef (mainly veal), goose, lamb, venison, and chicken were the most popular used for feasting. If born into a large wealthy household, then you could expect the larger cuts of meat, but for the poorer folk (the majority) then meats such as chicken, rabbit and possibly lamb were alternatives. Only the richer folk could afford to roast or spit their joints, and boiling was the preferred method for poorer people as it ensured all the meat was used and there was little in the way of waste. Even the bones of the animal would be chopped to release the nutritional marrow, something these days we prefer to feed to our dogs!

Whenever possible people cooked outdoors, as this prevented the home from becoming smoke filled and was less of a fire risk.

Richer folk would employ a cook, usually male, and may have also had a baker and dairy person, usually female. It was not unheard of for the kings of Saxon times and before to call in outside caterers. These were people paid to cook various dishes on the day of the feast. It's amazing to think that the average burger van is continuing such an ancient custom! Bread would have constituted the bulk of the meal, with the normal unleavened or flat bread being replaced with raised, possibly incorporating fruits and spices for the occasion.

What people ate then largely depended on their location and what was seasonally available. For example, if you lived near the coast then you would expect fish and other sea food to make up a large part of your diet. Similarly, if living inland on poor soil, then you might expect more in the way of rye bread, pulses and nuts to make up your diet. For the majority, food consisted of bread and poorer types of meat such as pigeons, hedgehogs, etc. Birds would sometimes be baked encased in their own clay wrap which served two purposes, one that it ensured the bird remained whole throughout cooking and the other that the clay once removed took the feathers with, it saving them the job of plucking fiddly birds.

Although we may squirm at some of the foods and methods of cooking, we must remember they knew no different, and apart from times of famine and poor harvest, probably enjoyed a healthier lifestyle.

From dental evidence of over one thousand years ago it seems our ancestors knew little of sweet things, and even by Anglo-Saxon times these were rare luxuries not eaten to extremes, as it was thought too much in the way of sweet-meats led to gluttony.

In these times of childhood dental decay and increasing diabetes, we could do well to emulate some of the more appetising aspects of our ancestors' diets. The most likely sweets consumed on wedding days were milk custards with fruits, much like our modern egg custard tart.

They used whatever herbs and spices were available locally, but great store was set by them both for their healing abilities and for their ability to season and flavour foods which otherwise could be virtually unpalatable.

One of the most prized possessions in Tudor times, and before, we presume, was pepper. This humble seasoning cost the earth as it had to travel from the east to reach our shores, and if you had it in your larder you were wealthy indeed.

Salt was more readily available and used for preservation of meat, hence salted meat was the most commonly consumed. It would have been soaked in fresh water for many hours—sometimes a whole day—until as much salt as possible was removed, and then chopped into small pieces and added to the proverbial stew. This stew formed the basis of the diet and was cooked in large pots or cauldrons made of iron, or copper if you were rich. Cooks of the time needed strong arms to lift these great weights, especially once filled.

Breads and sweetmeats could be cooked on flat pans (not dissimilar to frying pans) laid directly on top of the fire under the main cooking pot. Apart from the very rich, nearly everybody was involved in some way in the production of food and drink, which was the most important consideration. They don't seem to have worried too much over the amounts and there is little evidence for any careful weighing of ingredients where the common folk were concerned, but cooks working for lords and kings would have had scales to weigh ingredients out, as they had more to play with in the first place. It seems to a large extent the majority of our pagan ancestors cooked by eye and experience.

They did concern themselves with quantities of fuel required, and in one recorded event from Anglo-Saxon times it is noted that they reckoned on about 15 cwt of fuel for 120 lb of pig to be used. The fuel used for the cooking pot or spit would be whatever was locally available, with woods of all types being the most popular. Wood was still in surplus supply in most areas of Britain, and all wood burns, but they weren't wasteful. The better timber was kept for building and only the brash or ends of the tree was bundled into faggots for burning. Charcoal was also produced and used for fuel, again using the poorer quality wood not suitable for other purposes.

Some parts of England had suffered from deforestation by Tudor times, mainly due to ship building and general use, so peat was dug and dried for burning—something that continues in parts of Ireland to this day.

There were several beverages consumed by our ancestors: water, milk or whey, ale, mead, fruit juices, wine and herbal infusions. Wine was the highest on the list with water at the bottom. I think it highly likely that richer hand-fastings would have almost certainly drunk wine, with the poorer folk sticking to mead or apple cider brewed especially for the day. It is important to note that our native ciders are generally very high in alcohol, with Cornish scrumpy thought to be the strongest and not the innocent fruit juice you may presume. A friend of mine fairly new to this country allowed her twelve year old son to buy some cider to drink with his friends, not realising it was an alcoholic beverage. You can imagine the consequences! Whoops.

It would be virtually impossible to exactly replicate an ancient pagan hand-fasting feast, but we can copy it to a certain extent without upsetting your guests gastronomically.

People always remember the food so, even if your budget is low, allow for this—and why not have fun anyway making some of it yourselves? It doesn't matter whether it's from an expensive delicatessen or pulled up from an allotment. As long as it is well prepared and relatively neutral it will go down well. Hot and spicy food may well be very popular these days but it doesn't seem suitable as wedding food, so unless you know for sure that everyone coming will love it then its best avoided.

Finding out in advance if you are catering solely for vegetarians, or omnivores as well, is a good idea bearing in mind that to be accurate historically then meat or fish would have to be the focal part of the feast. For our ancestors the feasting part of the celebration was the main event, but sadly in many cases these days we seem to have put alcohol above this and reduced the meal to a limp buffet.

It is perfectly possible to feed your friends well and supply them with enough falling-down water to reduce even the most stoic guest to giggles without it having to cost the earth.

For real authenticity I would advise you purchase only the best quality organic free-range meat available, with wild boar, venison and fresh fish being very much top of the medieval pops.

It may not be possible for you to cook your feast on the day itself, or you could be a tad nervous about cooking traditionally over an open fire. Either way it is always possible to prepare the meat in advance and have it cold on the day.

Before we look at some of my personal suggestions for your hand-fasting feast, let me state categorically that unlike my daughter I am not a qualified chef. My suggestions are just that, suggestions. For accurate recipes and cooking times it would be best to consult any of the recipe books I have recommended in further reading to avoid potential disaster!

In keeping with our ancestors I have little in the way of accurate measurements and weights, preferring to just give basic guidelines on amounts and how long to cook them. Our ancestors may have laid the basis for today's plethora of culinary expertise but they were more concerned with using what was readily available to its limits, without any waste, than with the artistic displays of cuisine we have become used to.

Thankfully many twenty-first century chefs are returning to a more rustic form of cookery, where the quality of ingredients used and simplicity of cooking is of more importance than presentation, hurrah!

Loaves

Bread was the staple diet globally for most people two hundred years ago and back as far as five thousand, so it should form a part of your feast.

The best quality bread would be baked for the occasion and artistic shapes including those of knots would be created. The bread would be leavened or yeast risen white bread, with herbs and seeds included such as parsley, thyme, marjoram, cumin, caraway, and poppy among many others. You can obtain interesting and flavoursome breads from most bakery sections of today's supermarkets or bake your own if feeling capable.

White wheaten flour was considered the richest treat, and therefore any white crusty loaf will do. It is nice to warm the bread before serving and traditionally it would be broken into chunks and served with whatever meats were available. Potatoes largely replaced bread as a starchy accompaniment after Tudor times, but to be true to our pagan ancestors we should use bread as well as or instead of potatoes.

Sweet breads were also used to add bulk to the feast and provide variety. These were white breads with small pieces of fruit baked into the loaf. These can be purchased from most larger supermarkets. If not, try making your own and adding spices such as nutmeg and cinnamon. These can be served with a spoonful of organic honey, the only real source of sweetening available to our ancestors.

Trout and New Potatoes with Green Salad

Fish isn't everyone's cup of tea, but if you are planning two dishes as a main meal it is a very good choice for one dish. The fish can be obtained fairly cheaply, either by catching them yourself or buying direct from a troutery or fishmonger.

Ingredients

Trout

Fennel
Sea salt and pepper
Olive oil
New potatoes
Green leaves
Olives or hazel nuts
Nasturtiums.

I would allow 1 lb of trout between four people. The fish can then be simply cooked wrapped in silver foil over any fire or barbecue. I would stuff mine with fennel (picked from the garden or bought) and season with sea salt and freshly-ground black pepper. By drizzling some virgin olive oil over the fish and sprinkling more sea salt over the top, you should get a slight crust to the skin. They only take about ten minutes each side to cook, depending on how hot your fire is and how large each fish is, so check after eight minutes just in case.

I would try to obtain some fresh new potatoes from either an organic gardening friend or alternative organic supplier. Most modern supermarkets sell organic fresh produce now, but it is expensive. My supplier grows his own and has an honesty box outside his house. These people are usually easy to find if you live in the countryside, but if you are in town you will have to rely on what is available. I would slightly parboil the potatoes the day before and just heat them through on the day in a pan of boiling water with a little fresh lemon balm thrown in.

You can use any fresh green edible leaves you want, but a nice combination if you can get them is baby spinach, basil, red cabbage and nasturtiums. Wash all the leaves except the flowers and place in a large bowl. Pour on a reasonable amount of dressing of your choice or, to avoid sogginess, have it as a separate option. Dress with flower heads and a few black olives or nuts, and season.

Cooking fish in this way is a modern adaptation suitable for our barbecues. If you want a more genuine ancient flavour, then poach the fish in skimmed milk with a smearing of butter afterwards. The herbs used were most probably sorrel, fennel and a garnish of fresh watercress, especially in the southern wet areas.

Hog Roast

This is a firm favourite of the ancestors, but very difficult to manage unless you have the setup required. As I mentioned earlier it was mainly an autumn or winter dish, but there is no reason nowadays why you can't have it for your hand-fasting at any time of year.

You will need an awfully large barbecue or fire to spit-turn a hog roast and plenty of strong arms to turn it. There are small businesses that operate hog roasts at festivals and county shows, so it might be possible if the budget allows to hire one of these outfits for the day, totally in keeping with the behaviour of kings of old.

An average hog (wild boar being my favourite) will take many hours to cook and needs constant basting, but is well worth the effort if served with plenty of salad or vegetables. You can just serve chunks of meat in a bun if you want, but look into the feasibility first before getting carried away.

As a general rule allow twenty minutes of cooking time per pound of meat, plus thirty minutes. Make sure you get your fire good and hot and allow about twenty inches between hog and fire, with the hottest part of the fire required nearest the haunches where the bulk of the meat is found and takes longest to cook.

A good charcoal fire will take *at least* thirty minutes to get up to heat and you are looking for white-hot wood or charcoal, not leaping flames that will singe but not cook right through.

Have a long skewer handy to poke deep into the flesh to check if it is cooked through. If the skewer comes out cold and when removed the flesh bleeds, then it is not cooked through. Making a basting brush out of a bundle of rosemary tied to a stick, and a delicious pre-prepared baste from melted butter, salt, pepper and garlic to marinade with, is great and really brings out the flavour of the meat.

Venison

This lordly meat is entirely appropriate for a wedding feast and can usually be found available in most rural areas. To cater for a large number of guests the whole beast may be required—but be warned: it is not cheap, apart from during culling season in the autumn, when it should be a tad cheaper.

Venison should have been hung for several weeks before cooking and care should be taken with ensuring this is so, or you might end up with very tough meat. If you really like the idea of using venison but are on a budget, then venison sausages as an accompaniment to either pork or beef is a good idea.

Venison can be roasted in the same way as any other meat and because of its strong flavour is unlikely to need any marinading, but using the same basting method as hog roast would be delicious. We had it for our last winter solstice meal and served it with roasted parsnips, blanched sprouts and roasted garlic bulbs with a rich gravy made from the juices of the meat—and Yorkshire puddings, of course!

As a rule venison requires twenty five minutes per pound plus twenty five minutes, and an additional ten minutes if cooked covered in foil.

Goose

This would most definitely have been a popular choice for feasting due to the sheer numbers of them kept by the ancestors, but not necessarily for hand-fasting unless held in winter months, the traditional time for eating goose.

It is a fatty bird, though, and not considered suitable for those watching their weight. For this reason it requires very little additional fat to cook in.

It's not to everyone's taste, though, so check first and provide an alternative dish for those not keen.

As with any fowl, goose can be spit-roast, but you may require several for a large feast. I personally would avoid this method as goose is fatty and drips profusely, which smells unpleasant over an open fire.

As a basic guide, cook it for the same time as you would turkey but use less fat. I would serve it either with a fresh spring salad or with roasted root vegetables, depending on the season. Younger birds only need fifteen minutes per pound plus an additional fifteen minutes, with older birds requiring slower roasting allowing one and a quarter hours for the first pound and twenty five minutes for each extra pound on a lower heat.

Salmon and Pasta

Fresh pasta
Cooked salmon
Pine nuts
Dill
Fresh garden peas
Lemon
Salt and pepper.

Decide in advance how much pasta you will need. Simmer for three to five minutes in salted water then drain. Add chopped cooked salmon, pine nuts and peas. Garnish with dill and a squirt of lemon. Season to taste.

This gives you a simple dish that you can prepare in advance and one that, with the exception of the pasta, is traditional for this country. Salmon was a common fish to use at feasts for the common folk, with pike being reserved for the rich. Personally I think the poor got the better deal but some would disagree.

If you want to be more authentic then use a mixture of pulses, beans and nuts instead of the pasta.

Cold Ham and Salad

By purchasing a pre-cooked large leg of boiled or roasted ham you can save yourself many hours of cooking and preparation. This works well with all types of cooked meats and can be served with a variety of optional side dishes.

I would try to make sure there was enough bread for everyone and add salad leaves and pre-cooked beans and pulses with mixed fresh herbs, oil and seasoning. By including locally found nuts and fruits you will be copying in essence the ancestors' cooking methods without having to scour the countryside for ingredients not readily available.

Vegetarian Feasting

Many people these days are committed vegetarians and pagans are no exception. For the poorer of our pagan or heathen ancestors, who made up the majority of the population, meat was a luxury and many had to rely on vegetarian foods making up the bulk of their diet. Pottages of all sorts were the most popular, and these could range from a thin vegetable soup to a rich broth or stew of vegetables and pulses.

Although it was unlikely that a feast would be exclusively vegetarian, that doesn't mean we can't use the methods employed to create a vegetarian dish suitable for your hand-fasting and your vegetarian guests.

There is a running joke amongst friends of mine who have lived on protest sites and in communes that once you have one vegetarian in your midst then you all invariably end up eating vegetarian. This is because almost everyone will be prepared to eat tasty veggie meals but you will never get the vegetarian to eat meat.

These days it makes sense to avoid much of the meat on the market, from a pagan perspective. If we are to revere mother earth and all her creatures how can we justify eating conventional factory-farmed hormone- and additive-ridden meat that comes from unhappy animals forced to live an unnatural life for our benefit? So without droning on about unethical meat production let's look at a couple of vegetarian alternatives.

Vegetable Stew with Rosemary Dumplings

Although we do eat meat in our family this is one of our favourite vegetarian dishes. Allow about 1 lb of vegetables per person.

Potatoes
Swede
Carrots
Cauliflower
Onions (one onion per 2 lb of vegetables)
Garlic (one clove per 2 lb of vegetables)
Oil or vegetarian butter (2 oz per 1 lb of vegetables)
Seasoning (to taste)
Vegetable stock (about 1 pint per 2 lb of vegetables)
Vegetable bouillon (about one tablespoon per 1 lb of vegetables)
Dumplings or crust (for quantities follow instructions on suet packet)
Vegetarian suet
Flour
Salt and pepper
Finely chopped rosemary
Water

Wash, peel and chop all vegetables to roughly the same size, fairly small. Using a large cauldron or pot, add enough butter to sauté them in and melt. Add salt and pepper. Add chopped onion and garlic. Soften until lightly golden. Add chopped vegetables. Allow them to sauté in butter, adding more if required, keeping a close eye out to avoid burning, and turn occasionally for about twenty minutes over a low heat. Add stock and bouillon. Put on lid and allow to simmer gently for up to three quarters of an hour, making sure the vegetables stay firm. Make up dumplings or dough as per normal, adding the chopped rosemary to taste. Ideally you want to see a few flecks in each dumpling—not too much, as it can be over-powering. Remove cauldron or pot lid. Add dumplings to top of stew about twenty minutes before serving, or roll out to form a crusty lid. They are done once they go a golden brown on top and have a crusty outside with a light and fluffy inside.

This can be served by ladle into bowls with hot crusty bread.

Vegetarian Kebabs

Shallots
Courgettes
Peppers
Tofu pieces pre-marinaded in a mix of soy sauce or a rich vegetable stock.
Vegetarian cheese

Allow enough for one kebab per person.

Wash all vegetables. Peel outer layers of shallots or small onions. Slice courgettes into chunks. Cut peppers (I like to use a mixture of red, yellow and green) into chunky pieces. Slide these alternately, including the tofu pieces, on to your kebab sticks. Cook over barbecue or fire, turning frequently until all the vegetables are cooked. It doesn't matter if they become a little singed on the edges—it adds to the taste. Grate cheese and sprinkle a small amount over top of each kebab just before serving, so it just starts to melt. You need to be careful with this as if it melts too much it ruins the effect. Season and serve hot.

A Herb Most Sacred

Allium sativum or garlic, as it is more commonly known, is very much a food we either love or hate with equal passion.

This most sacred of herbs was used by most of the ancestors for flavouring and medicinal uses. I make no apology for including it in some of the above recipes as it deserves to be there. In its freshest and purest form, garlic leaves no odour on the breath, so cooking it alone is often a good way of taking it. Our British ancestors would have used wild garlic with its spring onion type of bulb and pretty white star flowers. It makes a new and enlivening addition to any savoury dish. Whatever you do don't go pulling up wild garlic from private land without permission.

Although it is thought to have originated from Siberia, garlic can now be found growing over almost the entire globe, with the French being most famous for using it. Up until the fifteenth century it had humorous associations, being thought to promote laughter by its consumption. In ancient Egypt it was once used as a form of currency and many of the pyramid builders were fed large quantities due to its ability to fend off disease. Even the ancient gods and goddesses of ancient Greece and Rome either loved it or loathed it: Circe feared it and Ulysses made use of this fear by waving it in her face to escape from her. Throughout history it has been used as both a love potion and as a means of warding off the evil eye. Hence the association with vampires!

It strengthens our immune systems, thins the blood, wards off mosquitoes and gnats, is disputably an aphrodisiac and, most of all to those who love it, tastes sublime.

So for all the above reasons it occurs in these recipes, but for those of you who loathe it then just substitute it for spring onions or strong shallots.

Dairy Food

Milk products were widely consumed by the ancestors with cows' milk being most highly prized. Full-cream milk was rarely drunk, as it was considered too rich for human digestion and a waste.

Semi- or fully-skimmed milk or whey was the most commonly consumed, with goats' milk used for invalids and poorer people, and ewes' milk in sheep country such as Wales.

Butter was churned and salted heavily to preserve it, but was used sparingly as it was quite a luxury.

Cheeses of all sorts were made but hard cheese was a favourite as it kept longer, with cream cheeses being eaten in early spring when there was a glut of milk available after calving and lambing.

Simple custards were popular and would have probably formed part of the feast dessert created from curds and whey with egg and spices. They differed slightly from those of today, but having custard tart for pudding would be most appropriate for a Beltane hand-fasting.

A Lammas or summer hand-fasting could use seasonally available fruits such as apples, blackcurrants and blueberries, with a soft sponge summer pudding and cold egg custard being very in keeping with days of old.

To make a simple egg custard for four people (you can multiply the ingredients for larger numbers or make several custards) you need two large free-range organic eggs, one tablespoon of caster sugar, three quarters of a pint of fresh semi-skimmed milk and a nutmeg to grate over.

Beat the eggs and add the sugar and pre-warmed milk.
Stir for a few minutes to allow the sugar to melt, but don't let the milk get too hot or boil—the eggs will curdle if you do.
Pour into a pre-greased dish and grate some nutmeg on top.
Stand the custard dish in another slightly larger one half filled with water, and bake in the centre of a low oven (275–300°F or gas mark 1–2) and cook for one and a quarter hours.

An alternative to this dish is an egg custard tart where you place the custard in a dish containing pre-cooked shortcrust pastry.

Simnel Cake

Warning this is a very nutty cake. For those allergic to nuts choose a rich fruit cake without them instead.

8 oz almond paste
6 oz butter
6 oz honey
grated rind of half a lemon
1 oz ground almonds
7 oz plain flour

1 oz cornflour
1 level teaspoon of mixed spice
3 eggs
1 tablespoon brandy (optional)
12 oz currants
2 oz candied peel
1 egg white

Roll out half the marzipan to 7 inches diameter.

Mix butter and honey, add lemon rind and ground almonds.

Sift plain flour, cornflour and spice, and add to creamed mixture.

Add fruit and candied peel.

Put half mixture into pre-greased 7 inch tin.

Lay rolled marzipan on top.

Add rest of mixture.

Bake in centre of moderate oven (325°F, gas mark 3) for 2–3 hours.

When cool, smear with honey, add other half of rolled marzipan, and brown under a grill.

Dust with icing sugar and sprinkling of cinnamon.

Serving dishes and implements

Even by the bronze and iron ages, wood was the most readily available material for cups, platters and dishes for the poor, unless they lived in a clay area and had access to cheap pottery.

Pewter became more popular and readily available by medieval times. I wouldn't advise you to use old pewter as it contains high quantities of lead, so use modern pewter—it's much safer and if kept clean can shine as well as silver, hence it's previous reputation as the poor man's silver.

If authenticity concerns you, then using wood, pottery, bronze, iron or pewter would be totally in keeping.

Forks are a relatively modern invention. Our ancestors just used a knife and fingers to eat, so you can follow this tradition if you wish. But bear in mind some people might have difficulty with it, and have a few forks handy just in case.

For those on a northern path, drinking horns are entirely appropriate and can be for individual use, or communal use if you have one large enough to pass around. The rest of us can use wooden cups (without handles—they were more like little bowls), pewter or ceramic, as glass didn't make its appearance in everyday use until much later in our history. If you have a large enough goblet it can be used as a loving cup for the couple to drink from first, whilst it is then passed ceremonially around your congregation. You can use glass, though, as it might be your only option, especially if you are dealing with large numbers, and many companies rent them out for special occasions.

Traditionally a man would prepare the feast, with women being responsible for the beverages, which you can also emulate if you wish and probably do already without realising it every time you have a barbecue!

Drink

If you already indulge in home brewing of any type, whether of wine or ale, then I expect you will be creating your own special hand-fasting brew.

But if not brewing specialists in your own right, then enlist the use of someone you know or can be recommended to you for the occasion.

I am not going to attempt to give anyone instant brewing lessons, as I wouldn't really know where to start and there are a great number of books available for you to read already on the market, but I have included a mead recipe at the end of this chapter. What I will say is drink whatever you like, but if your hand-fasting is to be of the spiritual type then showing reverence to mother earth by only buying organically produced beverages will show the greatest respect—and they taste better, too.

Most off-licences and supermarkets sell organic wine and beer that can be used, and is not that different in price from the alternatives more commonly bought these days. It is nice to find what is available on your doorstep and searching out smaller breweries can be very worthwhile, as can attending any of the many real-ale festivals held around the country. These can be useful sources, often allowing you a taste of what's on offer before you buy.

Spirits and all their many derivatives are fairly modern inventions and not really suitable at hand-fastings, but often find their way in, frequently in someone's pocket! I wouldn't worry too much about this. It's not worth getting sanctimonious about.

I personally would opt for copious quantities of honey mead and a good quality red organic wine, with non-alcoholic organic fruit juices and fresh mineral water as alternatives for those who want them.

Simple Recipe for Traditional Honey Mead

4 lb of honey (can be purchased from local beekeeper or commercially)
Champagne yeast
1 gallon of spring water

Dissolve honey in 4 pints of water and bring to boil for fifteen minutes.
Skim off white surface scum.
Add rest of spring water and pitch at room temperature.
Rack off when fermentation slows down.
Bottle once settled and clear.
Age up to three years but can be drunk earlier.

Remember to use sterilised containers to avoid contamination.

Serve as it is or add freshly cut slices of orange for a particularly luxurious taste.

Another traditional inclusion at any hand-fasting would be a large bowl of clean fresh water for guests to wash their hands in prior to eating. Our ancestors did this, and it makes perfect sense, so give people the opportunity to do so before eating and it will become a part of the ritual of the day. This can be romanced for the occasion by the addition of suitable aromatic flower petals in the water, and don't forget to have a couple of hand towels ready for people to use afterwards.

6

Preparation

Try to account for everything before sending out invitations, and adjust as required. You might find the day you would like is not the day you can afford and need to compromise in some way. It is possible that you already have a good idea about how much you have to spend on your day, so stick to this and, whatever you do, don't allow yourselves to get into debt with it. By running through this check list well in advance you will be able to get a picture of how much your day will cost before spending a penny. If compromises have to be made don't despair, as a hand-fasting really shouldn't cost the earth. You can cut corners by emphasising the spiritual aspect, and be cheeky by asking everyone to bring their own picnic, and just provide the drink yourself. I know a couple who opted for this route and no-one thought any the less of them for doing so. We all had fun sharing each other's food and ate very well, with them providing a barrel of ale to keep our spirits up. There are always ways to economise and the more you can make or prepare yourself the cheaper it can be. For example, don't go to expensive lengths over flowers. Just cut some of your own from your garden or a friend's. I won't advise you to deliberately desecrate our hedgerows since this is illegal, as is the picking of many of our wild flowers, so unless you know for sure the difference between those you can pick and those you cannot then leave well alone. Obviously the more time you have to prepare, the longer you have to make things for yourselves, so try to be patient and not rush into it. This very special day is about the joining in love (and spirit) of two souls, not about showing off to friends and outdoing so and so's hand-fasting. In essence it's your hand-fasting, not anyone else's. Try to remember this if things start to balloon out of control, giving yourselves reality checks as required. It's often the little things that make a day special, so pay attention to the details. Your truly loving friends and family won't care if it ends up a meagre affair, as the spirit of the day is about love and sharing.

Hand-Fasting Planner

The following pages have been left blank for you to use as your own personal planner, with key words to help you. Where the word budget appears it offers you a reality check and encourages you to compromise if needed financially on the less important details.

Spiritual Path/paths

Priestess or priest or celebrant
Telephone numbers and addresses

Traditions

Customs and practices to be included

Ceremony format

Order of service
Helpers and their roles
Telephone numbers and addresses

Gods or Goddesses

Spiritual energies/deities

Offerings

Budget
Choosing what is appropriate

Which season?

Moon phase
Date and time

Venue

Where?
Booking required?
Budget
Telephone numbers and addresses

Invitations

List
Telephone numbers and addresses

Binding method and material

Clothing and Accessories

Where from?
Budget

Catering

What kind of food and drink?
Budget
Who to do it?
Telephone numbers and addresses

Altar

Flowers and decorations

Rings and things

Budget
Where from and what types

Cake

Where from?
Budget
Telephone numbers and addresses

Entertainment

Budget
What kind? If any
Telephone numbers and addresses

Hair and personal grooming

Personal gifts to each other
Budget
Telephone numbers and addresses

Travel

Budget
Guests
Telephone numbers and addresses

Photography

Budget
Telephone numbers and addresses

Honeymoon

Budget
Telephone numbers and addresses

Thank-you letters and gratuities

Telephone numbers and addresses

End Note

If you have the time, shop around for the best deals but make sure everything can be done in plenty of time. You don't want to order a new gown for the day only to find it cannot be finished until after your hand-fasting. This goes for everything really.

If you both lack organisational skills or become overwhelmed by it all, there are usually family members and/or friends only too willing to take over some of it, so pass your tasks around. Then all you have to do is check up on them and write down their achievements in your planner.

As you can see from their roots, hand-fastings are very open affairs with the minimum of rules and regulations.

It would be a sad day if hand-fastings and other pagan rites of passage came under some sort of all-encompassing definitive law. Due to the fluid evolving nature of paganism, I think this highly unlikely although some paths, Wicca in particular, are beginning to show very early signs of this. I hope most practising Wiccans can remain true to their own individual path and not feel the need for direction and guidance in a set and structured way over everything, which I feel would limit future personal growth.

I understand that for any coven to work there has to be understanding and agreement over rites and rituals, but too many people these days are getting into paganism as a way of boosting their own egos and use it as an opportunity to 'priest it up'.

There was a couple I heard about several years ago who wanted to be hand-fasted but didn't know where to go or whom to ask. They announced their intention at their regular Moot and had several prospective priests and priestesses volunteer, anxious to see to their rite. This confused them further. One of the couple came to see me for a tarot reading and while with me asked whom they should have 'do it'. I asked her to forget the offers for a minute and just feel instinctively whom they would like to 'do it' if they could choose anyone. She suggested one of the women who hadn't offered, but was worried whether to approach her. I suggested she did.

She asked the friend she really wanted, who agreed nervously but was surprised and flattered that she had been chosen. Ironically this chosen one came to me for advice and we discussed various issues before she carried out the hand-fasting. It went brilliantly but, I suspect, the over-inflated egos of the original volunteers were not happy.

The popularity of hand-fastings is increasing daily for many reasons, one of those being the growth of interest in paganism, and another that they lack discrimination. For the latter of these reasons they have become attractive for gay couples to enter into, which is some compensation for the continued reticence of governments to allow legal marriages of this type. I am not about to get into the heavy politics of sexuality but it seems a shame that people don't get the chance to express their love and devotion conventionally if they so wish.

These days we consider marriage to be about love and commitment to each other and the legality of children has been relegated to a secondary issue. With the world's population still ballooning out of control in relation to the resources available, perhaps this is a valid evolution of marriage in the twenty-first century.

Hand-fastings are beautiful and magical days far exceeding any civil affair and well worth holding if you follow a pagan path or prefer a non-Christian alternative. I hope this book has provided you with ideas and inspiration for the planning of your hand-fasting and that you have enjoyed reading it as much as I've enjoyed writing it. Maybe once paganism is a recognised and acknowledged belief system, people will be able to have legally binding hand-fastings and save us poor pagans the trouble of having to hold two ceremonies! I look forward to that day!

In love be joined
On this merry day
Two souls as one
In their own way.

Sources

Pagan Federation
BM Box 7097
London WC1N 3XX
www.paganfed.demon.co.uk

The Order of Bards, Ovates and Druids
PO Box 1333
Lewes
Sussex BN7 1DX

Shelagh Gotto
Jewellery designer/maker
Handfasting rings
gottojewellery@aol.com

Morrigans Raven
Hand made ceremonial robes and incenses
www.morrigansraven.co.uk

Pans Pantry
Incenses, resins and rare gums
33 Damgate Street
Wymondham
Norfolk NR18 0BG

www.panspantry.co.uk
Caduceus
Specialist jewellers
35 Carnarvon Road
Leyton
London E10 6DW

Coppice Craft
Suppliers of natural wooden wands and besoms
10 Klondyke
Bury St Edmunds
Suffolk IP32 6DB
www.gaia.force9.co.uk

Ceilidh bands
Two web sites worth checking out
www.witchhazelmusic.co.uk
www.ftech.net/~webfeet/eceilidh/bands

Oakilia
Supplier of magical goods and services
Mole Catchers Cottage
North Road
Alconbury
Weston Huntingdon
Cambridgeshire PE28 4JZ
www.witchwaycrafts.co.uk

Bibliography

Folklore, Myths and Legends of Britain
The Readers Digest Association
Second edition 1977

The Druid Source Book
John Matthews
Blandford 1996
ISBN 0-7137-2572-9

The Penguin Atlas of British and Irish History
Various authors
ISBN 0-140-29518-6

The Druid Renaissance
Philip Carr-Gomm
Thorsons
ISBN 1-85538-480-9

The Year 1000
Robert Lancey and Danny Danziger
Abacas
ISBN 0 349 11278 9

Ritual and Desire
Catullus 61 and 62
Ole Thompson
Aarhus University Press
ISBN 87 7288 288 3

A Handbook of Anglo-Saxon Food Processing and Consumption
Ann Hagen
Anglo-Saxon Books
ISBN 0-9516209-8-3

Two Fat Ladies
Obsessions
Clarrisa Dickson Wright and Jennifer Paterson
Ebury Press 1999
ISBN 0-0918707-39

Magickal Weddings
Joy Ferguson
ECW Press 2001
ISBN 1-550224-61-1

Handfasted and Heartjoined
Lady Maeve Rhea
Citadel Press 2001
ISBN 0-8065-2194-5

Teenage Witch's Book of Shadows
Anna de Benzelle and Mary Neasham
Green Magic 2001
ISBN 0-9536631-5-9

Gourmet Cooking for Vegetarians
Colin Spencer
Andre Deutsch Ltd 1979
ISBN 0-8600720-35-7

In Search of England
Michael Wood
Penguin Books 2000
ISBN 0-140-24733-5

Wiccan Spirituality
Kevin Saunders
Green Magic 2002
ISBN 0-9536631-6-7

Alternative Weddings
An essential guide for creating your own ceremony
Jane Ross-Macdonald
Taylor Trade Publishing 1997
ISBN 0-87833-977-9

Guide to Wedding Vows and Traditions
Carley Roney
Broadway Books
New York
ISBN 0-7679-0248-3

Suggested Further Reading

Tree Wisdom
Jacqueline Memory Paterson
Thorsons 1996
ISBN 0 7225 3408 6

Sacred Celebrations
Glennie Kindred
ISBN 0906362482

Sacred Tree
Glennie Kindred
ISBN 0953222713

The Complete Dictionary of European Gods and Goddesses
Janet and Stewart Farrar and Gavin Bone
Cappall Bann
ISBN 186163 048 4

The Invitation
Oriah Mountain Dreamer
ISBN 0-722540-45-0

Wicca
Vivianne Crowley
Thorsons 1997

The Teenage Witch's Book of Shadows
Anna de Benzelle and Mary Neasham
Green Magic 2002
ISBN 0-9536631-5-9

Index

Green Magic Publishing

Green Magic Publishing is an independent publishing house based in the South West of England.

We hope you enjoyed reading Handfasting: A Practical Guide – our other titles are:

The Faery Faith – Serena Roney-Dougal
Reclaiming the Gods – Nicholas R Mann
Wiccan Spirituality – Kevin Saunders
Teenage Witch's Book of Shadows – Anna de Benzelle & Mary Neasham
Underworld of the East – James S Lee
The Lost Magic of Christianity – Michael Poynder
The Isle of Avalon – Nicholas R Mann

All Green Magic books are available either direct from your local bookshop or from our prime distributor, Counter Culture. Please contact Counter Culture at The Long Barn, Sutton Mallet, Somerset, TA7 9AR, Tel/Fax: 01278 722888 or email info@counterculture-books.co.uk

A fully illustrated catalogue of all Counter Culture titles is available upon request.

Green Magic is always interested in receiving manuscripts, especially in the fields on Magic and Wicca, Sacred Landscape and Spirituality.

Green Magic Publishing
BCM INSPIRE, LONDON, WC1N 3XX
TEL/FAX 01823 698895
www.greenmagicpublishing.com
email: info@greenmagicpublishing.com

THE FAERY FAITH
An Integration of Science with Spirit

Serena Roney-Dougal

Forward by Caitlin Matthews

The Faery Faith is a breakthrough book, which deals with a worldwide view which comes out of an ancient belief in Faery. A scientific spirituality with its roots in the Perennial Philosophy and the Great Chain of Being.

"Generations of folklorists have introduced us to the world of the fairy-folk. In a highly original step beyond, Serena Roney-Dougal relates it to many other things - magic, terrestrial magnetism, megaliths, apparitions, UFO reports - and shows how this Faery Faith can illuminate them all. To experience fairy reality, properly understood, is the key to a profound wisdom."

Geoffrey Ashe.

"A wise, intelligent and entertaining book from a unique and important teacher."

William Bloom.

"If you have ever sat in a beautiful spot in the countryside and felt within you a deep tug of something that was not quite memory, not quite recognition, but nevertheless was profoundly moving, you will enjoy this book."

Caitlin Matthews (from the Foreword).

'Highly recommended'

The Cauldron.

Serena Roney-Dougal is the author of the best-selling **Where Science and Magic Meet** (Element 1991) and (Vega 2002). She lives in Glastonbury, England.

The Faery Faith by Serena Roney-Dougal.
New Science / Spirituality / Folklore
Price £9.99 / $16.99   ISBN 0953663175 illustrated.

Reclaiming The Gods
Magic, Sex, Death and Football

Nicholas R. Mann

In the same way as the Goddess has been reclaimed in recent years, this book reclaims the God. Nicholas Mann, in this vibrant new work shows how the figure of the God has now become monopolised, marginalised and corrupted, to our great loss.

This is the definitive work on our lost gods, the gods of nature, animals, wealth, fertility, craft and inspiration: the loner, the trickster, the magician, the Green Man and the Wildwood King. **Welcome back the Gods of Old!**

In this lucid and original new work, Nicholas Mann establishes himself as one of our most provocative commentators on contemporary spirituality.

'A valuable and original work by a popular writer on contemporary spirituality'.   **Avalon magazine**

Listed as one of the **Bookseller's** New Age books of the year 2002.

Nicholas R. Mann is the author of many books, most recently **Druid Magic** (Llewellen 2000) and **The Isle of Avalon** (Green Magic 2001). He lives in Glastonbury, England.

Reclaiming the Gods by Nicholas R. Mann.
Mythology / Spirituality / Sexuality.
Price £9.99 / $16.99 ISBN 0953663183

Explained in straightforward language by a Wiccan High Priest, are the complete aspects of Wiccan practise. Meditation techniques, constructing an altar, working in a coven and circle casting plus the significance of Sabbats, rites of passage, the mysteries of the Elements and access to other worlds and everything you need to know to make magic work. This is a complete introduction to modern Wicca.

"An excellent summary of Wiccan ideas, very readable and accessible. A valuable addition to our library."
Museum of Witchcraft, Cornwall, England.

"Wiccan Spirituality is a concise introduction to modern Wicca, demonstrating clearly that Wicca is a modern spiritual path, of great importance today."
Pagan Federation, England.

Kevin Saunders is a visionary Wiccan practitioner who teaches at the Isle of Avalon Foundation in Glastonbury. He lives nearby.

Wiccan Spirituality by Kevin Saunders.
Magic / Wicca /Self Empowerment.
Price £9.99 / $16.99   ISBN 0953663167   Illustrated.

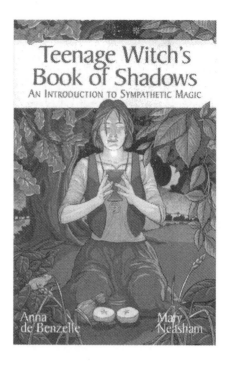

Green Magic is proud to have published this wonderful book. A genuine attempt to inform young people about Wicca amid its current high media profile. Others thought so too.

"This is a really great book providing the perfect introduction to sympathetic magic. The information is provided with humour and a lightness of touch in a friendly and reassuring way."

Mike Jones, Avalon.

"I really, really liked the spirit of the book. It introduces Wicca as a religion, not a game. It is full of useful information in a simple, easily understood form. It is the best book I have seen aimed at young people."

Mary Orchard, Silver Wheel.

"A superb introduction to witchcraft. Simple, straightforward and with a touch of magic."

Tyna Redpath, Goddess and the Green Man (Glastonbury).

"A valuable and interesting read, the links to websites are excellent."

The Triple Spiral

Teenage Witch's Book of Shadows by Anna de Benzelle & Mary Neasham.
Witchcraft / Self Empowerment.
Price £7.99 / $14.99 ISBN 0953663159

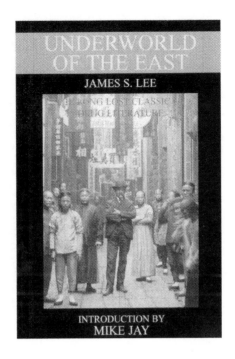

Green Magic received widespread congratulations for making this lost classic available to the modern reader.

The incredible story of James Lee and his adventures in the Far East in the early days of the last century. A fantastic tale of motorcycle gangs, man-eating tigers and drug taking on an epic scale. Excerpts recently appeared in the best selling **Dope Tales**. Ed. Howard Marks (Vintage 2002).

"One of the greatest works of psychoactive tourism ever written."

Michael Horowitz.

"Unusual for its time in its unabashed defence of copious narcotic consumption"

Times Literary Supplement.

"The publishers have done historians of medicine an immense favour."

Medical History.

"A wildly entertaining read. Strong drugs, back alleys and shady characters."

Beat Scene.

"A forgotten classic"

Time Out.

Underworld of the East by James S. Lee. Introduction by Mike Jay
Travel / Exotica / Drug Literature.
Price £9.99 / $16.99   ISBN 0953663116

The Lost Magic
of Christianity

Celtic Essene Connections

Michael Poynder

Lost Magic of Christianity is a startlingly original study of the Ancient Wisdom Tradition and Celtic Christianity in Ireland and the West. It unlocks the secrets of Stone and Bronze Age metaphysics that influenced the Gnostic practices of the early priesthood. These priests were vibrant seers, healers and highly skilled astromathematicians, expressing the oneness between human beings, nature and the living spirit of the Christ principle.

" An innovative and most unusual study of the Ancient Wisdom Tradition. A unique book."

Celtic Connections

"Seriously thought provoking reading"

Pagan Dawn

"Explains how ancient metaphysics encompassed knowledge of how to tap into energy flows and represent them in graphic spiral forms".

Nexus

Lost Magic of Christianity by Michael Poynder.
New Age / Spirituality / Ancient Mysteries.
Price £9.99 / $16.99   ISBN 0953663108   Illustrated

A fully revised and updated edition of Nick Mann's classic study of the mysterious and powerful Glastonbury landscape.

"Nicholas Mann explores Avalon in impressive detail."   **GeoffreyAshe.**

"Everything you wanted to know about the sacred mysteries of Glastonbury. Very nice it is too.".
Third Stone.

"Mann provides an impressive overview of Glastonbury's history and mythology. An enjoyable and valuable read".
Fortean Times.

Nicholas R. Mann is the author of many books, most recently being **Druid Magic** (Llewellyn 2000) and **Reclaiming the Gods** (Green Magic 2002). He lives in Glastonbury, England.

The Isle of Avalon by Nicholas R. Mann.
King Arthur / Celtic Wisdom / The Goddess.
Price £9.99 / $16.99   ISBN 0953663132   Illustrated.

Lightning Source UK Ltd.
Milton Keynes UK
UKHW022105251119
354217UK00008B/573/P